PONY
TALK

Also by Judy Richter

Horse and Rider
The Longeing Book

PONY TALK

A Complete Learning Guide for Young Riders

Judy Richter

Photographs by Philip Richter

HOWELL BOOK HOUSE

New York

MAXWELL MACMILLAN CANADA

Toronto

MAXWELL MACMILLAN INTERNATIONAL

New York   Oxford   Singapore   Sydney

Howell Book House	Maxwell Macmillan Canada, Inc.
Macmillan Publishing Company	1200 Eglinton Avenue East
866 Third Avenue	Suite 200
New York, NY 10022	Don Mills, Ontario M3C 3N1

Macmillan Publishing Company is part of the Maxwell Communication Group of Companies.

Library of Congress Cataloging-in-Publication Data
Richter, Judy.
    Pony talk: a complete learning guide for young riders / Judy
Richter; photographs by Philip Richter.
        p.   cm.
    Includes index.
    ISBN 0-87605-849-7
    1. Horsemanship.   I. Title.
SF309.R5   1992   92-31371   CIP
798.2'3—dc20

This book is not intended as a substitute for
professional advice and guidance in the field of
horseback riding. A young person should take
part in the activities discussed in this book only
under the supervision of a knowledgeable adult.

Macmillan books are available at special discounts for bulk purchases for sales promotions,
premiums, fund-raising, or educational use. For details, contact:

Special Sales Director
Macmillan Publishing Company
866 Third Avenue
New York, NY 10022

10 9 8 7 6 5 4 3 2 1

Printed in the United States of America

Contents

A Note to Parents

THIS BOOK is intended for youngsters who are just starting their riding careers. Zealous parents often want their children to start riding too young. I prefer to start riding lessons at about age seven, when the child has gained sufficient strength not to topple off if the pony sneezes. Also by age seven most children have started school and are ready to take instruction and are ready to learn to ride. With younger children a carefully supervised leadline ride on a quiet pony or sitting in front of an adult on a quiet horse suffices. If properly done that will spark children's interest, and they will feel more comfortable around horses and ponies. Remember that to a little child even the smallest pony looks gigantic.

Once a child has turned seven, has the coordination to ride, and is eager for lessons, then a parent has to search around for the best place for the child to start riding. If you are a parent who does not ride or know much about horses, then consult the Yellow Pages and visit some local stables. The best source of information, however, is the American Horse Shows Association, 220 East 42nd Street, New York, NY 10017-5806 (phone: 212-972-AHSA). This is a na-

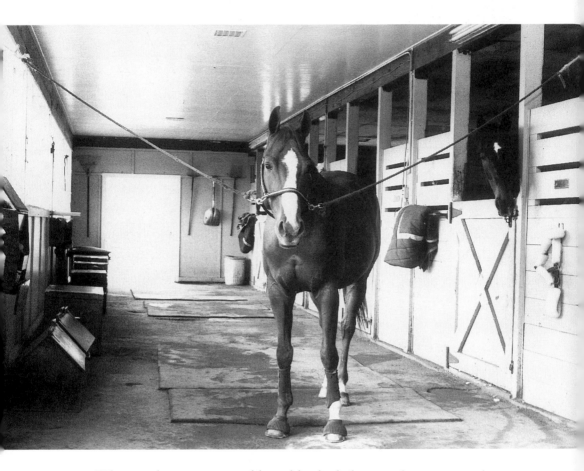

When seeking out a suitable stable, look for one that is neat, clean and workmanlike. The barn aisle should be free of debris and dirt.

The tack should be cleaned properly and put away neatly.

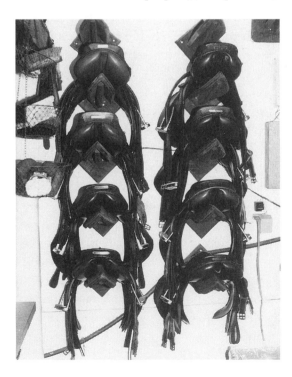

The ring where the lessons are given should show that whoever is in charge has some kind of plan. Here there are several little jumps in a definite pattern. Parents should seek out a barn where the child will learn more than just to steer a horse and post to the trot. Beware of rings that are overcrowded with horses and/or jumps. They are usually chaotic as well. On the other hand, children enjoy lessons with their peers, so do not select a place where there are no riders your child's age (unless you love everything else about the place!).

This is a carefully arranged, orderly ring. On the left side is a basic line of two jumps, one a vertical and one an oxer. The distance between the two jumps is 60 feet—a normal four strides. On the right side of the ring are three jumps—oxer, vertical, oxer—with 32 feet $+/-$ between them. Both lines can be jumped from either direction. In addition there is a single jump in the left corner which can be jumped alone or with part of the gymnastic. Numerous cavaletti are scattered about to be incorporated into various exercises. When space is limited, the jumps are set off the wall, so riders can work on the flat along the wall and avoid colliding with riders jumping. A well-planned ring is like a Montessori classroom. Students can work on their own and use the cavaletti and rails on the ground without interfering with lessons that are in progress.

tional organization, so no matter where you live, the AHSA will know of at least one good riding establishment near you.

Before you sign your child up, go and see the establishment, meet the instructor or instructors, watch some lessons and speak to other parents there. Most importantly, you must feel it is a safe place. If you observe situations that seem dangerous to you—youngsters on horses that seem too fresh, horses out of control, casual instructors—look elsewhere.

The stable itself should be neat and clean. "Glitz" has become very fashionable lately, but it is not at all important. Furthermore, it is expensive. A fancy place often masks considerable mediocrity. Several rings full of all the latest jumps and a barn full of brass and chrome can fool someone who doesn't look beyond the surface. A workmanlike barn will serve your purposes much better, for you want your child to be a horseman, not just a rider. The place itself will tell you a lot about the instructor. Even a parent who knows nothing about horses can tell if the horses are well cared for. Are they clean and well fed? Are the stalls and yard neat and clean? If the instructor is a poor caretaker and a slob, his or her teaching will also be mediocre and sloppy. Horses and riders alike will not ever "be all they can be" in such an environment. If you have a bad feeling about the place, trust your instincts and look elsewhere.

Recently I judged a horse show and gave a clinic in Alaska. To my surprise there was not just one but numerous good riding establishments in that state. Not only are they good, but now with the proliferation of satellite dishes, people there see more Grand Prix than I do and are current on what is happening throughout the horse world. So even in somewhat remote areas you will find a quality school.

Speak briefly with the instructor. Make it a habit from the start not to monopolize his or her time. The focus should be on your child's interest, ability and goals. Likewise encourage your child to "fit in," to accept the discipline of the trainer. You will sense right away if this is the kind of person you want your child to associate with and be influenced by. Remember your child will absorb a lot more at the stable than simply learning to ride a horse. The instructor is responsible for your child's safety and progress as a rider and as a person. Be realistic about finances. Riding and showing horses can be a very expensive sport. If the instructor has some notion of your financial commitment, he will be able to guide you so you will do as much as possible for your child, but remain within your means. You are doing your child no favor by overextending your finances and laying a guilt trip on him or her for your extravagance!

Riding is a sport in which women may and do compete with men on an equal basis, even at the Olympic level. As youngsters, girls sometimes catch on more quickly than boys, probably because they are not distracted by other sports, especially soccer, baseball and football. By the time children are competing at horse shows, the girls usually outnumber the boys and often win those early competitions. At this point we do lose a lot of boy riders, the ones who hate being beaten by girls, but the ones who truly love it and stick with it end up as very good riders. Riding is certainly no "sissy sport" at any level, so encourage boys not to give up for that reason. Be sure there are other men and boys riding at the place you select for your son. He needs some good role models, or he will soon lose interest and join his friends on the soccer or football field.

Learning-disabled children benefit tremendously from learning how to ride. A kindly horse soon becomes a wonderful and patient friend. The discipline of the lessons, learning diagonals at the trot, and leads at the canter, helps them manage difficulties with handedness and coordination. Just simple exercises like making sure their hard hats and boots are in the car ready for the lesson help them learn to plan and organize their lives. I personally know many learning-disabled children who have become excellent riders and great people as well. If your child has a learning disability, be sure to let the instructor know so he or she can make appropriate adjustments to your child's program. Most trainers have pupils with learning disabilities and are well able to help them become good riders.

For physically and emotionally handicapped children horseback riding can be an excellent sport and great therapy as well. For information about riding programs for the handicapped in your area, contact the North American Riding for the Handicapped Association, P.O. Box 33150, Denver, CO 80233 (phone: 1-800-369-7433).

Acknowledgments

For helping this book happen, my thanks to:

◇ Cullen Latimer, for demonstrating throughout.

◇ Brooke Hodgson Latimer, Cullen's mother, for her advice and support.

◇ Denise Ryan, my right hand, for typing and helping with the manuscript.

◇ Madelyn Larsen, my editor "extraordinaire," for her encouragement over the years.

◇ My family—husband, Max, and sons, Hans and Philip—for their staunch support always.

◇ Last, but by no means least, Frosty Lad, for his years of patience teaching dozens of children, starting with my son Philip many years ago, how to ride well. This book is dedicated to him and many unsung heroes like him who for centuries have helped riders be at once humble and proud.

Frosty Lad and Cullen are our demonstrators for this book. Cullen has been riding for a couple of years. Frosty takes the credit for teaching her everything she knows. Notice his bridle has been put on correctly and is properly adjusted. The bit almost makes a wrinkle at the corner of his mouth and the noseband is just under the bone on the side of his face. The bit and the noseband should not be too high nor too low. If the bit is too low he may get his tongue over it, and once started, it is a bad habit that is hard to break.

Introduction

A Few Words from the Pony Himself

HELLO! My name is Frosty Lad, and having taught many, many children to ride over the years, I feel that now at age twenty-five, I am somewhat knowledgeable in the subject. I urge anyone serious about riding whether for pleasure or in competition to try to think from the pony's (or horse's) point of view. Right away your "horse sense" will help you out. You will know you have to kick your pony along as you are leaving the barn (or going away from the ingate) and be ready to slow him down going toward the barn (or the ingate). "Home" is very important to all ponies and horses; we love the comfort of our stalls, our dinners waiting for us, etc. Whether walking, trotting, cantering or jumping, most of us, nearly all of us, want to go faster toward the barn or "home" than away—regardless of whether our riders are beginners or Olympians.

Remember ponies and horses are individuals like people. We all have our idiosyncracies, and each of us is different from all others. You will find that most of us are generous and forgiving. Some of us are unfortunately the helpless victims of bad treatment, and we all react differently to abuse. While some of us become very timid and untrusting; others lash out in anger, biting and kicking at all humans because some have abused us. We all rely heavily on our instincts. If startled, our natural reaction is to run away or lash out. That is how we survived for centuries as wild animals and our natural instincts are still with us. The best riders are true horsemen who learn to understand the animals in their care and know how to persuade their horses to do what they want them to do whether it is to take the proper canter lead or jump a 7′ Puissance wall.

Hope you enjoy learning to ride!

"Good Luck."

Your pal,

FROSTY LAD

PONY TALK

Chapter 1

Getting Started

L EARNING TO RIDE is not easy, but it is lots of fun. What makes riding more fun than any other sport is that you are involved with a pony or a horse. Every equine has his own personality, his odd little ways and certain things that he does well or does not do well. The best riders are those who understand their ponies or horses and are able to persuade them to do what they want them to do. Cruelty or abuse does not get it done, nor does overindulgence, that is, "spoiling." Ponies and horses do best when they understand their job. The good ones want to do it right. The spoiled ones and the ones with bad characters do not. There are only a few of the latter. Most ponies and horses have good characters; some, of course, are more generous than others.

Dress: Proper and Safe

Once you and your family have decided where you will take riding lessons, you will need to make sure you have suitable clothes and equipment. The correct attire for riding includes the regulation hard hat/helmet (approved by the American Horse Shows Association) that fits properly with a chin strap snugly adjusted. Never ride without one. Girls should develop early the habit of putting their hair up and wearing a hair net once they have passed the pigtail stage. (See the photographs in Chapter 4.)

The second "must" for riding is a pair of shoes or boots with heels. Sneakers and other flat shoes can slide through the stirrup with the result that the rider could be dragged to death by a frightened pony. (In my barn riders who "forget" their boots have to ride without stirrups that day. The good news is that riders will develop a good tight leg whether they want to or not.)

Attire should always be neat and clean, with the shirt tucked into correctly fitting jeans or jodhpur pants. For basic lessons and pleasure riding jeans are appropriate at most stables. Riders who are very keen and ride often can buy leather chaps to use every day to prevent their legs from becoming chapped. The chaps, whether ready made or custom made, are available at most saddlery shops. For example, Miller Harness Company (235 Murray Hill Parkway, East Rutherford, NJ 07073; phone 201-460-1200) can give you the name of a saddlery store near where you live, so you are safely and correctly dressed for your first lesson.

Special Needs

Here are some hints for cold-weather riding. Sheepskin-lined boots are warm, but remember that they must have heels and must be able to move freely in your stirrup irons. If they are too wide, you risk getting your foot caught in the iron, which can be dangerous. At winter horse shows wear a pair of rubbers with sheepskin or heavy felt innersoles over your regular riding boots for extra warmth. They can be removed just before you enter the ring. When taking a lesson in cold weather, don't wear a huge, fat goose-down parka that prevents your instructor from seeing your upper body. Wear a vest or windbreaker under the parka so you can shed the latter after the first few minutes when you have warmed up.

Veteran horse show riders always bring a warm parka, good raingear and rubbers to every horse show even on the warmest, most sunny day. Benefit from their experience of freezing and/or getting soaked and develop the habit early on so you do not suffer likewise. Rubbers save a lot of wear and tear on your boots, so always keep them handy. Even the early morning dew on the grass is hard on your boots. They are expensive, so take good care of them from day one. Never leave the barn or the horse show without cleaning them first. You will soon learn that dry boots polish up much better than ones washed at the last minute. This kind of attention to detail is what separates world-class riders like Michael Matz from the others. His daily example taught my son more effectively than years of his mom's nagging.

Tacking Up Your Pony

Many stables have the ponies all "tacked up," that is, saddled and bridled for their riders when they come for lessons. Make it your business to find out how to saddle and bridle the pony properly. Watch others tack up their horses and ask them to show you how to do it. Everyone needs to know the basics of stable management. Who knows? You might have a pony or horse of your own to look after someday! Of course, you want to be able to do it correctly, for it is a big responsibility indeed. M. Stoneridge's book, *A Horse of Your Own*, explains clearly all the details of stable management.

The photographs show that Cullen understands the basics of stable management. First she leads the pony, Frosty Lad, out of his stall and crossties him in the aisle in front of his stall. Next she curries and brushes him and also picks out his feet. The latter is most important. Possibly a rock is wedged between the shoe and his hoof. The bedding from his stall will be packed in his feet and must be cleaned out daily. Otherwise "thrush," a disease that is basically hoof rot, can develop.

The Saddle

Next she puts the saddle pads on his back, first a Navajo, or "Indian pad," then a foam pad, and finally the saddle and girth. She is careful not to make the girth very tight all at once. Some horses and ponies have "cold backs" or are "cinchy." If cinched up too suddenly they react by bucking and thrashing around. Some of the best and kindest

Here Cullen shows the proper way to lead a pony. She is on his left side. With her right hand she holds the rope close to his chin and with her left holds the end of the rope so it does not trail on the ground.

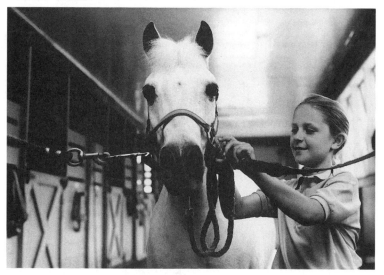

Cullen is crosstying Frosty so she can groom him and "tack him up," that is, put on his saddle and bridle.

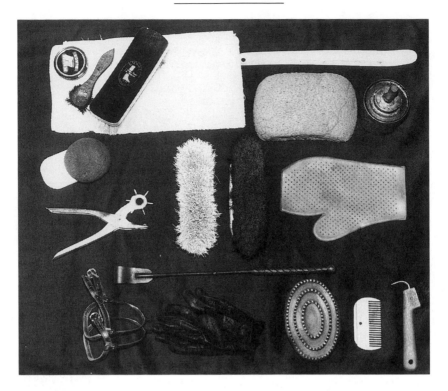

Cullen has laid out the equipment she needs for herself (leather hole punch, boot polish and brushes, gloves, stick and spurs) and grooming tools for her pony: curry comb, two brushes (stiff and soft), mane comb, rub rag, saddle soap and sponge, mitt, sponge and scraper for washing the pony, hoof pick and hoof dressing.

Here is how to use the equipment for grooming: (1) Use the *curry comb* with a circular motion to loosen dirt and hair. (2) Use the *dandy brush* (stiff bristles) and then (3) the *body brush* (soft bristles). Brush the hair in the direction it grows. Brush tail hair gently so as not to pull it all out! (4) Smooth the hair down with the rub rag (great use for old towels). (5) Use the *hoof pick* to pick out his feet before and after riding. Use the brush end to remove mud caked on the outside of his feet. (6) Apply *hoof dressing* before riding to dress him up and after to keep his hooves from drying out.

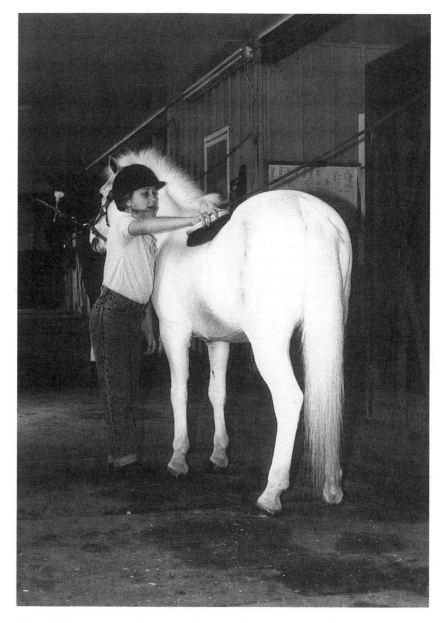

First Cullen curries Frosty with round sweeping strokes to loosen the dirt and hair. Now she brushes him all over, head to tail, under his belly and down his legs, being careful to brush in the same direction that his hair grows.

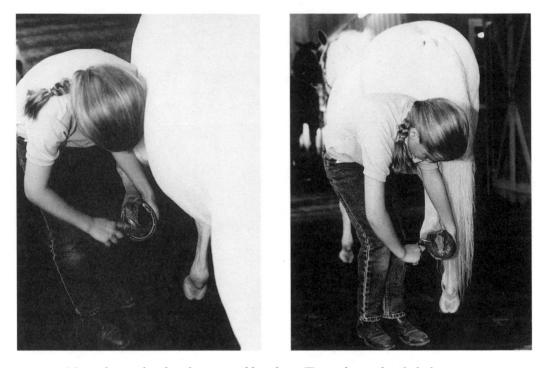

Now she picks the dirt out of his feet. To pick out his left feet, front and hind, she faces the rear, and runs her left hand down his leg to the pastern, the area just below his ankle and above his hoof. Next she leans her left shoulder against his left shoulder or haunch to shift his weight to the right side so he can pick up the left foot for her. The pattern is reversed when she cleans his right feet, front and hind.

Before she saddles and bridles him, she gets dressed herself. First the hard hat must be snapped in place. Harness hats are required by the AHSA (American Horse Shows Association) for all riders under 18 while competing at AHSA-recognized horse shows. This is a good rule, one to be observed by children and adults alike.

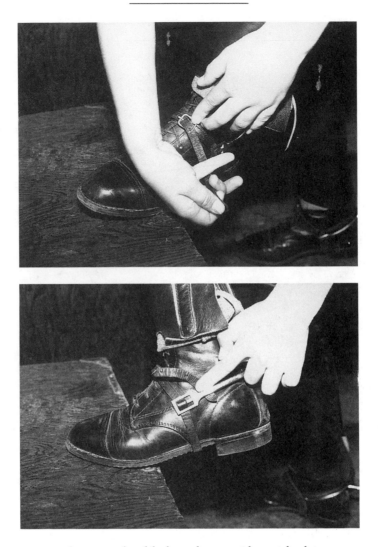

Next on are the spurs buckled to the outside, with the strap pointing down. If the strap is long, either cut it off or tuck it under the spur, so it does not flap sloppily against the boot. Some horses need spurs; others do not. Weather conditions are often a factor. Spurs are usually needed more in warm weather than in cold. Few horses need spurs in big open fields. Many need them in small and/ or spooky rings. Let common sense guide your judgment about the use of spurs. Use spurs only under your trainer's supervision.

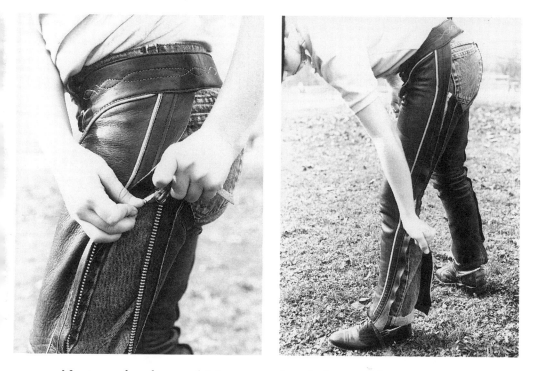

Next are the chaps, which are very handy for everyday wear. Made of leather, they can be ready made or custom made. They fit neatly over jeans and offer good protection to the legs. Riding just in jeans can cause sores on the knees and legs. (Jodhpurs and boots are always correct also.) The chaps buckle in front and zippers go down the legs on the outside. For riders who do all their own grooming and stable work, chaps are handy because they can be put on and taken off quickly and easily.

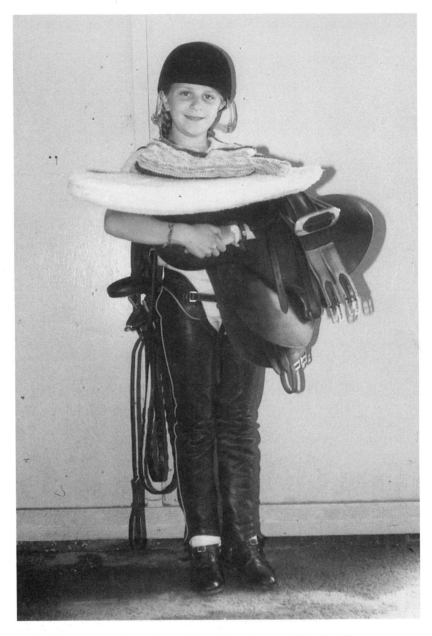

Now she is fully dressed, so she carries her saddle, bridle, martingale and saddle pads from the tack room out to the aisle where Frosty is crosstied.

After she folds the Indian pad, places it and the foam pad on his back, for protection, she sets her saddle gently down on top of them. Always put the saddle on before the bridle, so the pony remains crosstied and does not wander around the aisle and step on your toes as you saddle him.

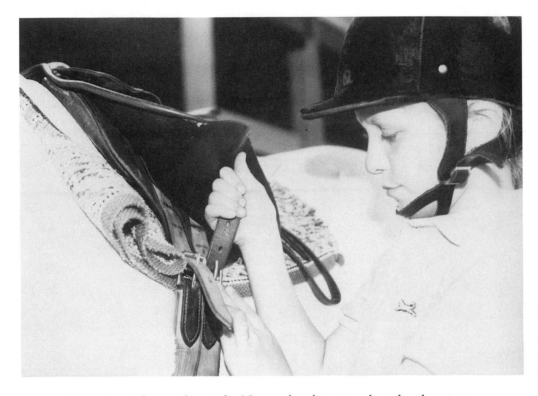

Next she tightens the girth. Not real tight yet—that she does just before she mounts. Some horses are "cinchy." Quickly tightened girths can make them very upset, so a wise horseman always makes it a habit to cinch up the girth slowly. Once mounted, the rider should always check the girth before starting the day's work. Most ponies and horses tend to "blow up," that is, puff out their bellies by holding their breath in an effort to prevent the girth being pulled tight.

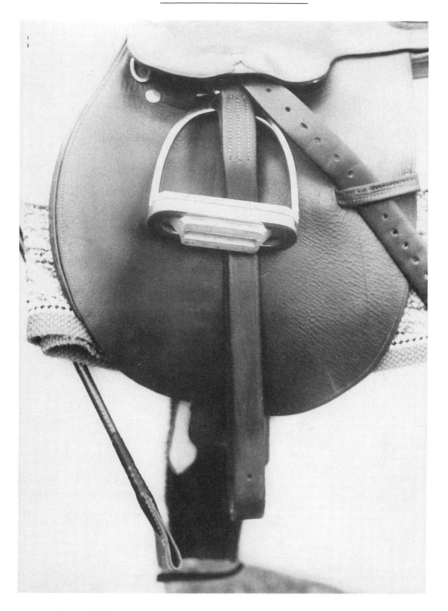

Here the saddle is in place with the stirrup irons pulled up and the stirrup leathers tucked in properly. Never leave the stirrups down because they can catch on something as the horse walks by or simply bang against his sides and startle him.

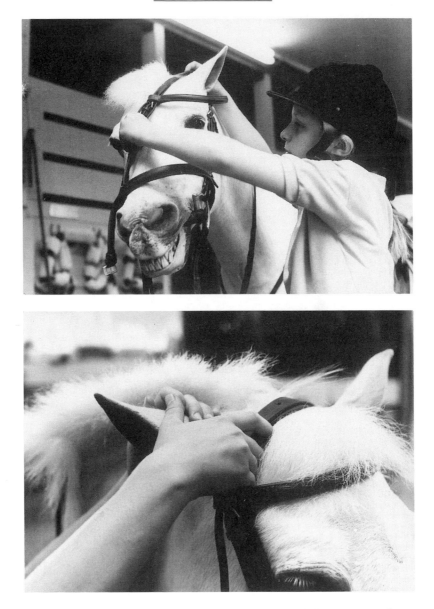

She slips the bit into his mouth first, being careful not to get her fingers between his teeth. Press his lip gently against his teeth to open his mouth if he resists. Next, she puts his bridle on gently over his ears, first left and then right.

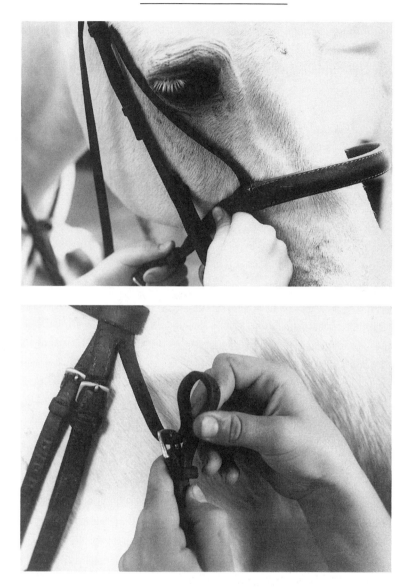

Now the noseband is tucked under the cheekpiece and buckled shut. Notice it is just under the protruding bone on the side of his head. And to finish, she buckles the throatlash shut: not too tight to choke him, not too loose to flap up and down. You should be able just to slip your hand between the throatlash and his throat.

Before mounting, she checks the length of the stirrups. When she puts her fingers on the buckle, the stirrup should reach almost to her armpit. At least now she knows her stirrups will be approximately the right length for her when she gets on. She may need to lengthen or shorten them just a hole or two, depending on the plan for the day's activity.

mounts that are otherwise always well-behaved are sometimes cinchy. Like people, ponies have their quirks. This particular quirk is easy to deal with. If it is overlooked, a serious accident can result. Therefore, it is a good habit never to make the girth very tight at first.

The Bridle

Be sure the saddle is securely on while the pony is still crosstied. Then put on the bridle. First put the reins over his head onto his neck so he can't escape. Then grasp the cheekpieces with your right hand and use your left hand to open his mouth. Put his lip over a tooth if he does not open his mouth for you. Then gently poke his ears—first left and then right—through the crownpiece. Finally buckle up the noseband and the throatlash. Allow four fingers' worth of space between his throat and the strap. Never crosstie to the bridle, only to the halter. That is the reason it is simpler to saddle him before bridling him. If you bridle him first, he may walk around—even on your toes—while you are putting the saddle in place.

Untacking

After your ride, lead him into the barn, locate his halter, remove the bridle and crosstie him. Then unbuckle the girth on both sides and put it across the saddle. Then remove saddle, girth and pads from his back. Put the saddle carefully on a saddle rack or lean it against the wall. Do not throw it on the floor and risk damaging the saddle tree. If it is warm, sponge him off and walk him until he is dry and cool. In chilly weather, rub him down with a rub rag. Before returning him to his stall, brush him, pick out his feet and oil them with hoof dressing. Then clean your tack.

Rugging Up

At night he may need a sheet and one or more blankets, depending on the weather. Again, common sense tells you how to "rug him up," as the British say. Allow for temperature variations in stables because some are much warmer than others. Also, the length and thickness of your pony's coat must be considered. Here are some guidelines. Regardless of whether you live in Alaska or Florida, if you are wearing a sweater, he needs a sheet; a jacket, he needs a blanket; sweaters and a down jacket, a sheet (next to his skin) and two blankets.

Mounting

Take the reins over his head and lead him from the barn to where you plan to mount. Make sure your girth is tight enough. Check your stirrup length against your arm's length as shown on page 18. Gather the reins in your left hand, stand by his shoulder, facing the rear of the pony, insert your left foot in the stirrup with your toe against the girth (not his ribs), grasp the cantle (back) of the saddle, and hoist yourself up. Be careful not to land hard on his back. Flopping on him may startle and even hurt him. In any case, it is a bad way to start your ride and your relationship

Though technically he is a "small pony" (12.2 hands and under), suddenly Frosty looks tall to Cullen, so she wisely seeks the mounting block *(see next page)*. Actually, any sturdy object serves the same purpose: a rock, fence rail, car bumper or whatever is handy.

Here she gathers her reins, making sure they are short enough to prevent his moving off when she is halfway up. Conversely they should not be too short, causing him to run backwards.

She puts her toe in the stirrup, pressing toward the girth so as not to jab him in the stomach and cause him to walk (or gallop) away . . .

. . . and swings her leg over to settle gently into the saddle. Ponies and horses hate it when the rider flops on their backs. It startles them and it hurts! There is no worse way to start the day.

When there is no mounting block handy, a helpful friend can give her a leg up. Again, she is careful to settle gently in the saddle.

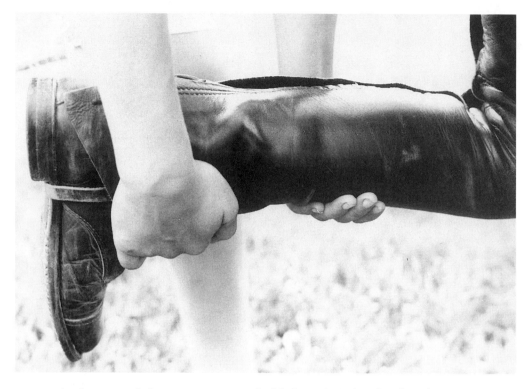

A close-up of the proper way to hold the rider's leg for the "leg up." Some prefer to jump on "one," others on "three." Learn to jump, so you are not like a sack of potatoes being heaved up on the pony.

Here she is mounting with the help of a lengthened stirrup iron. From early on, a rider needs to become self-sufficient. If no one is around to give a leg up and if there is no fence to climb onto, then the rider can always lengthen the iron and scramble on.

with him. If he is too tall to mount from the ground, use a mounting block or a fence rail, or even the bumper of a car to help you step up. Another option is to lengthen your stirrup to make the ascent less difficult. "A leg up" from a friend is another good way to get on your pony.

Stirrup Adjustment

Once mounted, double-check your stirrup length. With your feet out of your stirrups, the stirrup iron should be at the bottom of your ankle bone. To shorten or lengthen your stirrups, take the reins in one hand and keep your foot in the stirrup, as you adjust the length as shown in the photograph.

Dismounting

In order to dismount properly, take the reins in your left hand, quietly remove both feet from your stirrups and swing down. The reason for removing both feet from the stirrup irons is that you prevent the possibility of being dragged if you stepped down "cowboy style." Notice also how the stirrup irons are run up and the stirrup leathers are slid through. Always take the reins over the horse's head before you lead him into the barn.

Putting the Horse Away

Part of being a team player is making sure your teammate is put away properly. After you have finished your ride,

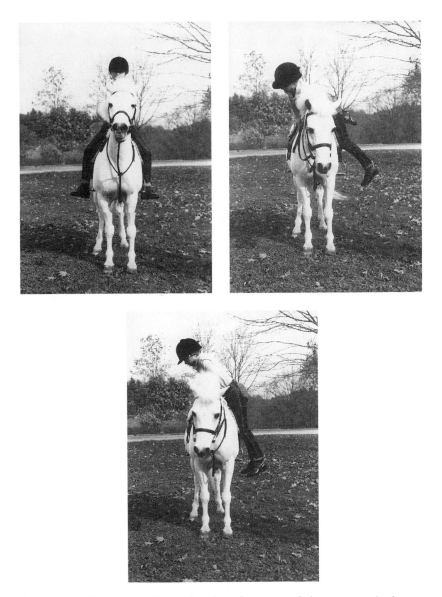

The proper dismount: She takes her feet out of the stirrups before swinging off. Leaving the left foot in the stirrup and dismounting "cowboy style" can be dangerous if the horse suddenly moves away. Develop the habit early on to drop both irons before dismounting.

After dismounting, Cullen slides the stirrups up the leathers . . .

. . . and then tucks the leathers inside the stirrup iron.

make sure he is not soaked with sweat and blowing hard when you return to the stable. If he is hot and blowing, walk him in the ring or around the barn before you bring him inside. Never put a horse away hot. If you do, you are inviting all kinds of problems, the most likely one being laminitis, or founder. Founder occurs when a horse's blood flows into his hoof faster than it flows out. The sensitive laminae are thereby destroyed and the bones in the foot become detached from the outer wall. A severe case is terminal. The horse suffers terrible pain and eventually has to be put down, all because someone was in too much of a hurry to cool him out properly. See the photographs on pages 36 through 40 for details on putting your horse away properly.

The Early Riding Lessons

The first few lessons you will be just getting your balance and starting to feel comfortable on your pony or horse. Most riding teachers start their pupils on a leadline until the student gets his bearings and understands the basics of controlling the pony or horse. The next step is usually the longe line, which gives the student more freedom but at the same time allows the teacher to stay in control. Because beginning riders are loose and awkward, a wise teacher does not release the lead or longe line until he is sure the rider is able to control his mount properly.

Correct stirrup adjustment: She has bridged her reins, keeping them short for control, and her eyes are up. She keeps her foot in the stirrup as she presses with her index finger the tongue of the buckle into the proper hole.

A close-up of bridged reins. When you need to have the reins in one hand, this is how to do it.

A close-up of the index finger pressing the tongue of the buckle into the hole. No need to look down. She can feel what she is doing.

Incorrect stirrup adjustment: Having dropped her reins, she has no control, which is a serious problem if her horse should bolt away. Her lowered eyes will not notice something that might be approaching and could startle him. With her foot out of the stirrup her situation is definitely insecure. Here is an accident just waiting to happen!

Correct girth adjustment.

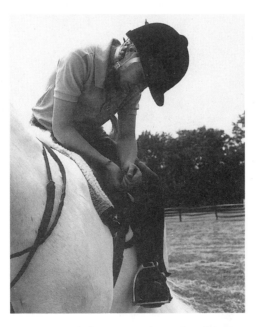

Incorrect (and dangerous!) girth adjustment.

Here she is leading the pony with reins over his head and stirrups properly run up. Safety is a prime consideration here as always. With the reins over his head, she has a lot more control should he scoot or shy. Stirrups banging on his sides could frighten him or get caught on something as they pass by. The best way to prevent accidents is make it a habit to do things properly in the first place.

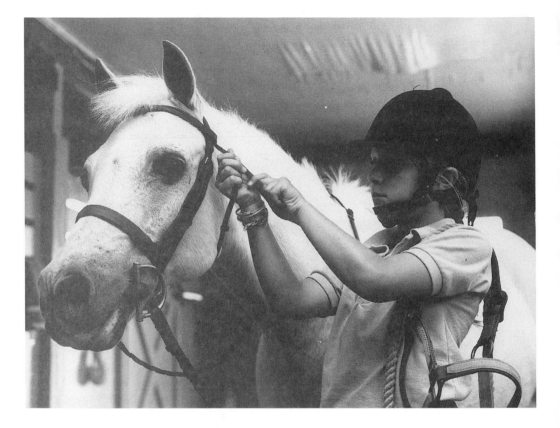

Now she prepares to untack him. Notice the halter on her shoulder, at hand so she can slip it on easily.

She slips the bridle off, but notice the reins are still around his neck, just in case he decides to try to escape.

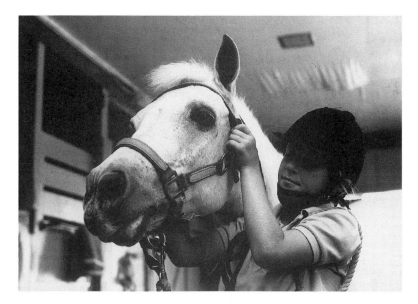

Now she puts on his halter. She removes the bridle first and crossties him before taking off the saddle.

Having located a friend to hold him, she sponges his neck and back with warm water. On warm days when the pony is sweaty, a sponge bath is the best way to get him clean. Use warm water always— unless the weather is very hot. If soap is needed, be sure to rinse it all out. Usually two rinses are needed to get all the soap out. On cold days, simply rub him down with a towel, and when he is dry, brush him well.

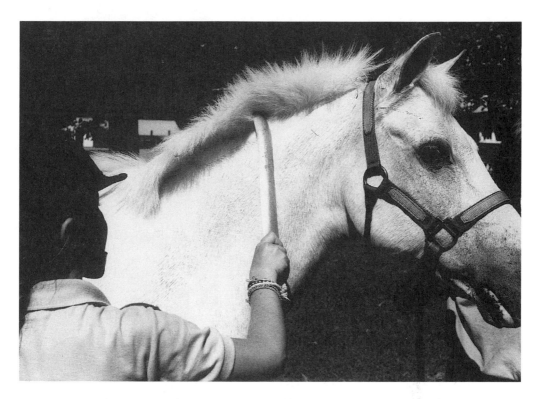

Next she scrapes the excess water off.

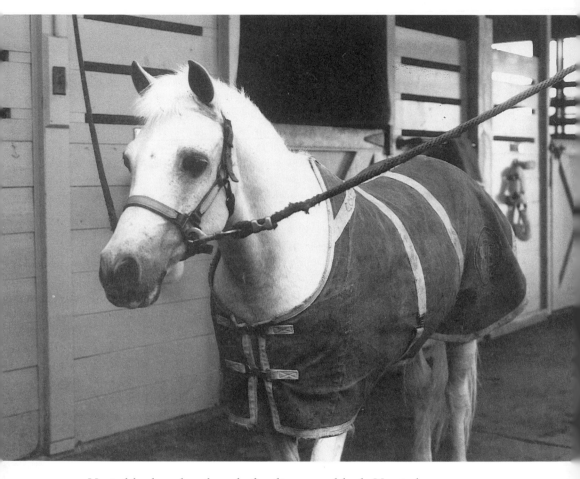

He is blanketed and ready for dinner and bed. Use judgment, depending on the weather. If you are in shirt sleeves, he probably does not even need a sheet. If you are wearing a sweater, put his sheet on; a windbreaker, his blanket; a down parka, several blankets. In deciding what he should wear at night, consider whether the barn is snug or drafty.

Chapter 2

Riding
on the Flat

F ROM THE VERY BEGINNING, it is important to concentrate on developing a good position. A good beginning in riding, as in anything else, can make all the difference later on. Develop good habits from the start and you will end up riding well. You have to check your position often until you become more secure in the saddle.

The Rider's Position

The proper basic position at the halt is to have head, shoulder, hip and heel all in line. Another imaginary line runs from the rider's elbow to the horse's mouth. Elbows should be just in front of the hips and hands should make an angle of about 45 degrees. About two-thirds of the rider's weight should be in the heels and one-third on the saddle. At the walk, trot and canter the rider's body should be inclined a few degrees in front of the vertical. Your weight should always be in your heels. A good exercise for even rank beginners is to stand in the stirrups and force the weight into the heels. A rider with a deep heel does not get ahead of his horse—a major fault that creates countless problems later. So get in the habit of having a good, solid, deep heel.

The Posting Trot: The First Big Milestone

You will probably start the posting trot on a leadline or longe line. At first you will not get it at all and you will bounce all over the place. Keep trying to feel the rhythm of the trot. It is hard to know how and when to rise. Let his trot toss you up. Suddenly you get it! Learning to post is like learning how to ride a bike. It is a major milestone, and once learned it is never forgotten.

Mastering Diagonals

The next milestone after learning how to post is mastering your diagonals. When a horse trots, his legs move diagonally: right front and left hind, left front and right hind. When the left front hits the ground, sit and you are on the left diagonal, and vice versa. Likewise when the left foot is up, you are up off the saddle. When going in a circle, as in

Here the rider is sitting correctly on her pony. She sits in the middle of him with her heel under her hip and her elbow in front of her hip. Her eyes are up and her shoulders are back. She has her weight in her heels as she should.

She is checking with her hand behind her seat to be sure she is not sitting too far back in the saddle. Sitting behind the center of gravity makes it difficult to be in harmony with the horse. Also, even a lightweight rider feels heavy to his kidneys, which are located just behind the saddle.

Incorrect: She is sitting on the back of the saddle with her feet out in front of her. She cannot be in harmony with her horse because she is behind his center of gravity and will always be "behind the eight ball." Her feet are so far away from his ribs that she virtually has no leg on her horse at all. Urging him forward from the leg is next to impossible when her feet are positioned like this.

Incorrect: Now her back is rounded. The slouch looks sloppy and *is* sloppy as well as ineffective. Anyone interested in showing in equitation classes with a rounded back like this will start her performance with at least two strikes against her. Such a sloppy look takes a lot away from an otherwise excellent performance.

Incorrect: Her back is too arched and very stiff. This position is equally unattractive and ineffective. Some trainers teach an exaggerated arched back, but it is only detrimental to a rider's look and performance. There are no good stiff riders.

The five rein aids. The direct rein is for stopping and turning. To stop, the rider pulls back on both reins and to turn he pulls back on only one rein.

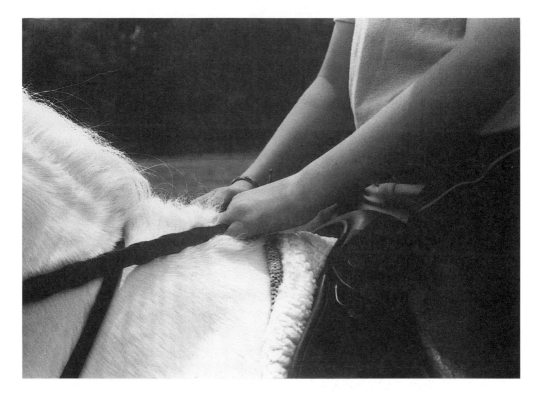

The indirect rein governs the horse's weight and/or bends his neck. It serves mainly to shift his weight from his inside shoulder to his outside hip as he is turning. Otherwise he will fall in as he turns. The indirect rein should not cross over his withers. If it does, your reins are too long! Here Cullen uses the indirect left rein to turn left smoothly and in balance.

The third rein aid is the bearing rein. Cowboys call it the neck rein. Use it to prevent your horse from falling out on his turns. Here she uses the left bearing rein to help turn right. Coordinating both reins and both legs is a key principle of riding.

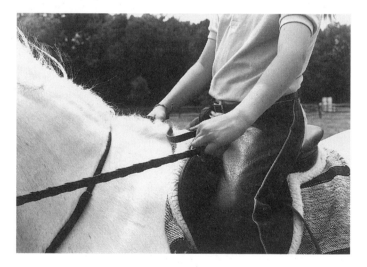

The leading rein does just that. It leads the pony to the left. It is used mostly on green horses and jumpers, and hence is not seen in the hunter/equitation show ring. Yet it is a useful rein aid that any serious rider needs to know.

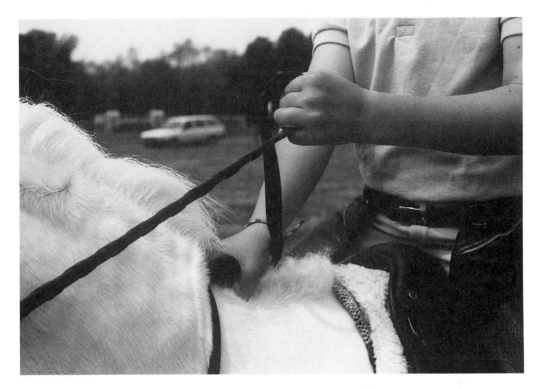

The pulley rein is a very important emergency aid to stop a pony out of control. Every beginner should know how to use it effectively. Cullen presses on his neck with her right hand for leverage and pulls with all her strength on the left—pulling him in a circle to gain control. Or, she can do the opposite: she can plant her left hand and pull hard with the right.

Correct leg and foot position: The stirrup is on the ball of her foot and her heel is down.

Incorrect: Her foot is "home," too far through the stirrup and her toe is pointing down.

Incorrect: Here she is too much on her toe and is in danger of losing the stirrup altogether.

Incorrect: Here her weight is too much on the outside of the stirrup.

She is "bridging her reins," putting both reins in one hand, (1) to free up the other hand to adjust stirrup and/or girth or (2) to use the crop.

Here she holds the crop correctly at the end and applies it correctly behind the saddle. Except for the occasional slap on the shoulder to straighten the horse, a rider should never hit the horse in front of the saddle. Hitting a horse between the ears or across the neck or face serves no purpose, is cruel and endangers the horse's eyes. Many horses have been permanently blinded by a crop across their eyes, an unforgivable sin for any rider to commit.

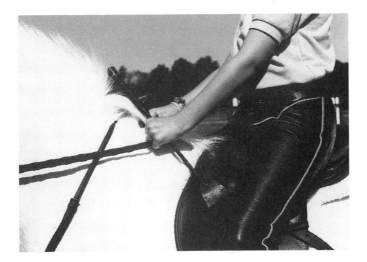

Incorrect: She is in danger of poking her own eye.

Her seat is correct. A conscientious rider checks her position often during the course of the ride. Checking the position often works better than trying to hold it every moment. The latter technique creates a stiff frozen look and no "feel." Feel what your horse is doing under you and adjust your position to accommodate him. Aim to be correct but not "frozen" in the saddle.

The big puffy down jacket prevents the teacher from seeing much of Cullen's upper body. Furthermore, as soon as she starts to work, she will be too hot. Never wear bulky coats and baggy sweaters in a lesson. Once you have warmed up, a vest or windbreaker is sufficient, and the teacher can see you much better.

Here she is looking down, which is totally unnecessary. This habit needs to be nipped in the bud. She must always look where she is going and feel what her pony is doing.

Posting on the correct, the left, diagonal on the track to the right. She is rising as his outside leg is off the ground. (The "outside" is always the side toward the rail. The "inside" is the side toward the center of the ring.) Here the pony is in better balance and she is posting just high enough, not exaggerating the post as in the next photograph.

Posting on the wrong, the left, diagonal. As his inside leg comes up, she is rising in the saddle while proceeding in a circle to the left. The reason this diagonal is incorrect is that when his inside leg is on the ground, bearing his weight, and she is sitting in the saddle at that moment, it must bear her weight as well.

Here she is "posting with the motion." The angle of her upper body follows the horse's motion. The rhythm of the horse's trot tosses her gently out of the saddle. There is no effort on the rider's part to throw herself up. Posting with the motion is the more natural post and the correct post for beginner and intermediate riders who need to learn to be in harmony with their horses.

"Posting behind the motion." Now her angle is very erect. Her back is perpendicular to the horse's back. This angle is suitable for dressage but not for intermediate hunter seat equitation. As the rider posts, she is driving her horse forward with her seat. Intermediate riders who post behind the motion end up being too stiff and rigid, losing the precious "feel" they should try to develop at that stage.

a riding ring, the correct diagonal is governed by the horse's outside leg. (The "outside" is the side toward the rail and "inside" is the side toward the center of the ring.) When his outside leg is up, the rider must be up. When it is down, the rider is in the saddle. Your teacher will tell you at first if you are on the correct diagonal. Then, gradually, as you become more secure at the trot you will learn to look over his shoulder to see which leg is going where.

The Canter

Once you are fairly secure at the posting trot, it is time to learn how to canter. Prepare your horse to canter by putting your outside leg well behind the girth to move his hindquarters toward the inside of the ring so he is properly balanced to strike off on the correct lead. The canter "lead" is called that because the horse leads with one foreleg. The correct lead occurs when the inside foreleg seems to step higher, that is, "leads." Once the horse is properly balanced with his hindquarters to the inside, press him strongly with your outside leg to get him to strike off on the correct lead.

Refinements

Eye Control

Beginners find it hard to know whether or not they are on the correct diagonal or lead. At first you will have to look

Cantering on the correct lead. Notice his inside foreleg leads.

Cantering on the incorrect lead. His outside leg leads.

down over the horse's shoulder to tell which lead or diagonal you are on. Next you can refine the look to a glance. Finally, you will learn to feel (and it is partly a matter of hearing) whether the lead or diagonal is correct. Feeling, instead of always looking down at your horse, is a good habit to develop early. You should not have to look at him to figure out what he is doing.

Focus on Your Destination

Practice looking where you are going. No doubt you have noticed that when people drive cars they do not look at the accelerator or the brake. They look where they are going (hopefully), and riders should too for all the same reasons. Eye control is another major milestone. Develop the habit of keeping your eyes focused on your destination. Horses have a way of "following your eye." For example, if you want to turn left, look first and then turn your horse. You will find that your turn will be much smoother if you look first. Just that little shift in emphasis and weight makes a difference to a sensitive horse, and you'll find he will indeed follow your eye. It may feel as though he is reading your mind, but by looking in the direction you want to go, you have telegraphed to him in a subtle way that you intend to make a left turn. By now you should be ready to ride off the lead- or longe line, and it is time to sharpen your skills.

Work on the Flat

Developing sound basics from the beginning makes achieving excellence later much more possible. Man has been riding the horse for eons, and our written records of the study of riding horses as an art goes back to Xenophon, a Greek historian who wrote about horsemanship in the fourth century B.C. Later, if you become truly devoted to the art of riding, you will want to read the many excellent books on the subject. For now it is enough to concern yourself with the basics, with developing a good position and proper control of your horse.

Schooling Exercises for Daily Flatwork

◇ *Ordinary trot to warm up.* Don't be too demanding the first few minutes.

◇ *Transitions through the trot (sitting, ordinary and strong trot) on circles and straight lines.* The sitting trot is slower than the ordinary trot, and the rider sits rather than posts. The ordinary trot is about 6 to 7 miles an hour. The strong trot is an accelerated extended version of the ordinary trot. Horses need to practice transitions from one trot to another in order to develop proper rhythm and balance and, most importantly, obedience to the rider's aids. Be sure the horse is straight on the lines and the arc of his body parallels the arc of the circles and turns.

◇ *Cantering.* A beginner usually uses the outside rein and outside leg to urge his horse into a canter. Later, these lateral aids are replaced by diagonal aids: the inside indirect rein to bend the horse slightly in the direction he is going accompanied by the outside leg behind the

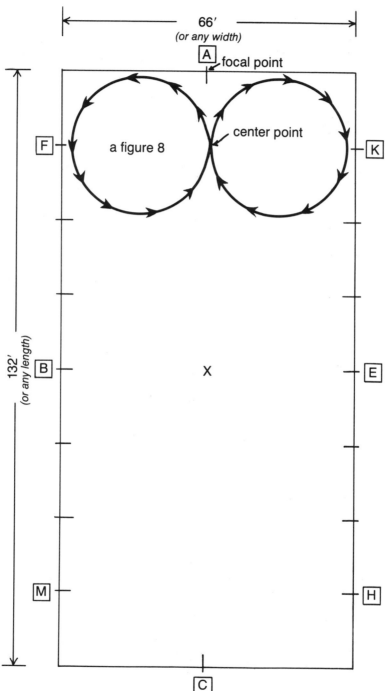

66'
(or any width)

A focal point

center point

F

a figure 8

K

132'
(or any length)

B

X

E

M

H

C

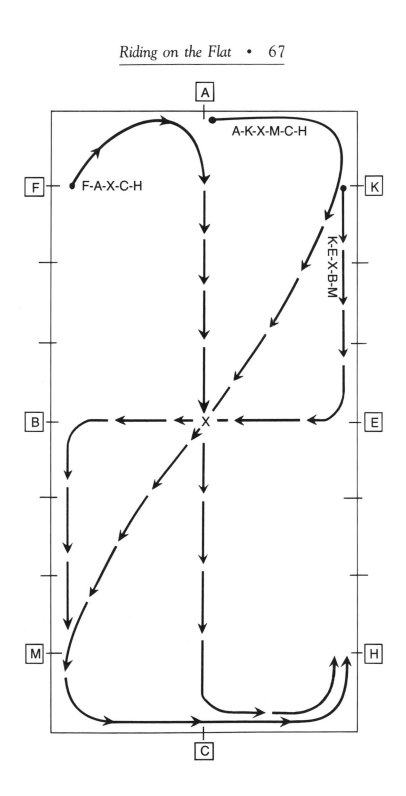

A-K-X-M-C-H

F-A-X-C-H

K-E-X-B-M

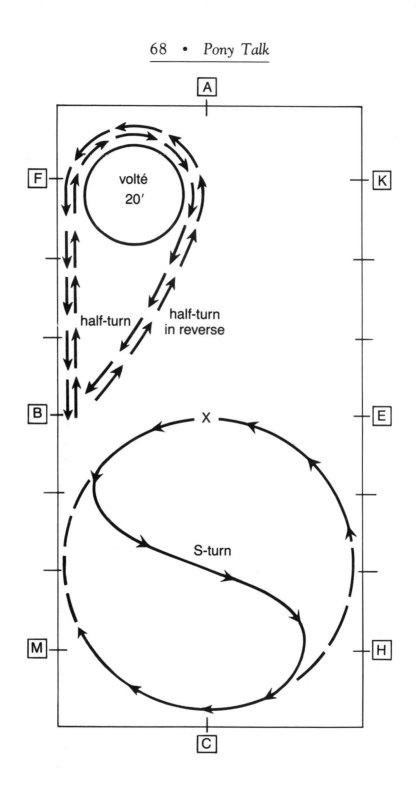

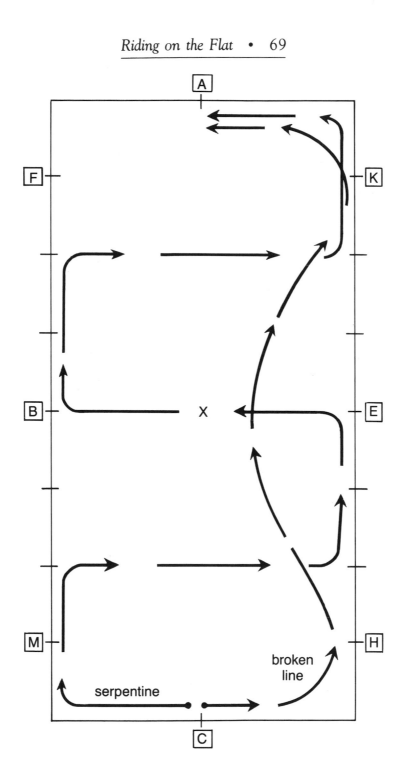

girth. (A gentle nudge with the outside leg before you actually ask for the canter will shift your horse's hindquarter to the inside so he is able to pick up the correct lead and will get his attention as well.)

Also, practice transitions between the ordinary and strong canter. The ordinary canter is the horse's normal canter, and the strong canter is slightly faster but is not a full all-out gallop. Cantering faster and slower teaches the horse to obey the rider's aids so that later the rider can adjust the length of the stride as he approaches jumps. A horse that is longitudinally adjustable, that lengthens and shortens his stride easily, has a tremendous advantage over one that does not. Some horses are naturally quite adjustable; others need constant training to help them respond quickly to the rider's aids.

◇ *Transitions from one gait to another, including the halt and the back.* Be sure to use both reins and both legs for all transitions, upward (faster) and downward (slower). Practicing transitions (that is, going faster and slower at each gait) is the best exercise for making the horse longitudinally obedient.

◇ *Halts.* Close both your leg and your hand to halt your horse to keep him still, immobile and straight. Stretch your back up as you close the leg and the hand. Do not allow him to overreact to your hand and back up.

◇ *Half-halts.* The half-halt is exactly that. The rider asks the horse to halt and, just as he is about to halt, rides him forward. The half-halt, though barely visible, is a simultaneous, coordinated action of the legs, seat and hands to get the horse's attention and to balance him before executing various movements or transitions to slower or faster paces.

The half-halt engages the horse's hindquarters and therefore lightens his forehand and his balance in general. Repeated half-halts are effective when the horse is too sluggish or the opposite, when he goes too fast. It is a quick, short gathering of the horse, an assertive signal from the rider to the horse to pay attention, to obey your commands.

◇ *Rein backs.* Less experienced riders tend to back their horses by using only their hands. More advanced riders close their legs as they close their hands to achieve a more balanced rein back. As the horse yields and backs a step or two, soften the hand. Don't continually choke him. This principle of rewarding the horse's correct response is an important one in the art of horsemanship. A rider who takes and takes but never rewards the horse's proper response soon will have an uncooperative horse on his hands. Whenever a horse reacts positively to the rider's aids, he must be rewarded or soon he will not react at all to them. And who can blame him? Why should he if there is no reward? Ask for a few steps at a time at first, and be sure to keep him straight. Don't back him every time you halt or he will learn this as his lesson and run backwards at every halt, a major disobedience.

◇ *Circles at all gaits.* This is an exercise in suppling and precision. Be sure the circles are round, not lopsided. The smallest such exercise, a volte, is a circle 20 feet in diameter. Circles are also good for settling a fresh horse or controlling a wild one. The S or serpentine turn through the circle, as from X to C, is one way to change direction: bending, then straightening one or two strides, and then bending in the other direction. Then open and close the circle at the trot and canter, using the same midpoint to teach the horse to stay in the "frame," between hands and legs. This exercise makes the rider deal with the horse's two major lateral evasions: cutting in or bulging out.

◇ *Changes of direction across the diagonal.* In your ring, for example, ride A-K-X-M-C-H, down the center line, F-A-X-C-H, or across the short side of the ring, K-E-X-B-M. Again, be sure the horse is straight on lines and bent around your inside leg on the turns.

◇ *Half-turns and half-turns in reverse, at all gaits.* For example, to do a half-turn proceed along B just past F right toward A (but never over center line A-X-C) and back to and past B. For half-turns in reverse, proceed from B toward A (but again not over center line A-X-C) and then left toward F and finally again past B. Changing direction develops a horse's lateral suppleness just as transitions in pace develop his longitudinal suppleness, and hence obedience to the rider's aids.

◇ *Neat, prompt departs into canter from walk.* The horse's

head should be bent slightly to the inside as you apply the outside leg. Here promptness and obedience are emphasized.

◇ *Free, ordinary, unhurried walk.* Allow the horse to stretch his head and neck. Use good judgment about giving him a break when working intensively on the flat. Ride and then relax. Ten minutes of concentrated riding is better than thirty minutes of purposeless meandering around the ring. Do not work your horse constantly; give him a little break every ten to fifteen minutes.

◇ *Turn on the forehand.* Do this one step at a time, not hurriedly. Your eyes should be up and your heels down. Novice riders can learn to perform the turn on the forehand, the first exercise in lateral movement for young horses and young riders. Hold your horse's head gently with the reins. Your inside leg should be on the girth, the outside leg pressing behind the girth to push his hindquarters around his stationary forehand.

◇ *Broken lines and serpentines at all gaits.* A broken line can be ridden, for example, from C and H toward X, then to K and A. This is a good exercise for practicing eye control: At H look toward X, as you reach X, deliberately shift your eyes to K.

Serpentine loops must match in length and width—another exercise in precision. Starting at C, proceed right past M across the ring to an imaginary point between E and H; at E turn left across X and right again at B; halfway between B and F turn right toward another imaginary point between E and K; proceed past K to A. The horse should be perfectly straight on the lines and nicely bent around your inside leg on the turns. Change diagonals and leads upon crossing center line A-X-C. Do simple changes of lead at the center.

◇ *Figure-eight at the trot and canter.* Practice nice round circles, holding the horse out on the circle and looking in to the center point for accuracy. The "focal point" is on the rail; the "center point," where the change is made, is about eighteen feet in from the rail, a little over the radius of the intended circle. For example, in the ring use as your center point an imaginary point about eighteen feet in from A. Facing A, your focal point on the rail, ride two perfectly round circles, one to the right, one to the left. At the canter, do simple or flying changes. A simple change can be executed either through the trot or the walk. (See page 75 for an explanation of flying changes.) If the horse anticipates change, halt four or five seconds between changes to increase his obedience to your directions.

◇ *Leg-yielding.* Leg-yielding is a basic exercise to teach the horse to be obedient to the lateral aids. It supples him and prepares him for more advanced lateral movements such as the shoulder-in. Leg-yielding involves bending the horse around the active leg, which pushes him away from the side where the leg is active. It can be done on a straight line, on a turn, on a circle or across the diagonal. At the turns, the rider can apply the inside indirect rein with an active inside leg, pressing the horse away from the inside of the ring. Be sure to keep the horse moving forward and be sure to prevent—with the outside leg—his haunches from swinging too much to the outside, an evasion common in many horses.

◊ *Flying changes.* Be sure the horse's body is completely straight before asking for a change. To teach him flying changes, shift hands to the outside of the turn to displace his weight from his inside shoulder to his outside haunch, meanwhile holding his hindquarters in with the outside leg as well. Then ask for the change with a strong outside leg. Do not let him increase his pace as you ask for the change. Use the rail or the wall of the ring to force the change and to prevent the horse from getting away from you. Nowadays, perfect flying changes on course are absolutely essential, even at the beginner and intermediate level, so take the time to learn to do them correctly and to teach your horse. Keep after him until he does them perfectly whenever asked. He may very well get upset until he understands what you want and has the coordination to do it. Don't be deterred by his getting in a flap, but on the other hand do not drill him until he is frantic. Be patient and use good judgment. A frantic horse cannot learn, so keep it simple and keep him calm. Stay calm yourself and persist until he learns it. The flying change should always be introduced and practiced at first under your trainer's supervision, for it is a difficult but very important exercise.

Remember as you are working your horse on the flat that he is an animal, not a machine. When you start, give him a chance to loosen up for a few minutes before you demand absolute obedience. Walk first for a few minutes (unless the weather is freezing cold—then trot right away! Again, good judgment is key!). A brisk trot in large circles and around the ring is a good way to start the day. During the course of your flatwork, take a break now and then. Let him walk on a loose rein, relax, and stretch his neck. He is not a bicycle, a tennis racket or a football; he is your friend. Keep it that way. At the end of your work, let him relax, and if your teacher gives you the go-ahead, maybe even take him for a stroll bareback. Obviously you need to have developed a secure seat and you want a quiet horse before you embark on a bareback ride. Safety and good sense must always come first.

Work on the Longe Line

The longe line is a very important piece of equipment for young riders to know how to use correctly. In the very beginning it is a handy and safe way to start rank beginners, as explained in Chapter 1. Intermediate riders should learn early on how to longe a horse, for it is the quickest and safest method for working down a fresh horse. If the wind comes up or the weather turns suddenly cold, quiet "fool-

Pony Back-Talk! A pony or horse that wants to buck like this needs a five- to ten-minute gallop on the longe line before a beginner climbs aboard. Even the very best ponies can get frisky now and then!

Here is how to attach the longe line to the bridle. Run the line through the bit on his right side, over his head, and . . .

. . . attach the snap to the bit on the left, the outside. Now you are ready to longe him to the left. To longe him to the right, (1) run the line through the bit on his right side over his head and snap it on the left side. Or (2) do the reverse.

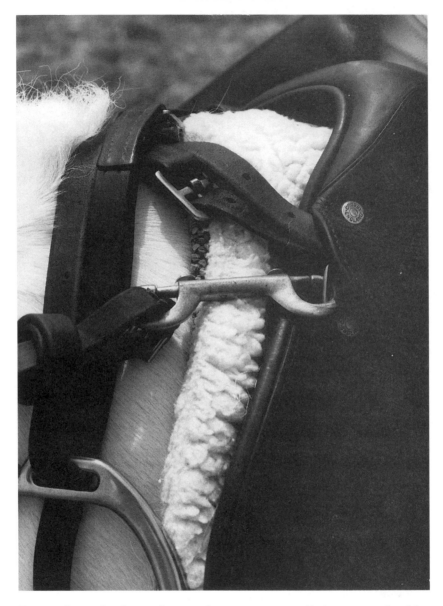

For work on the longe line without stirrups, pull the stirrup buckles down and cross. Snap the knotted reins to the saddle.

proof" horses and ponies can and do make liars of us all. They too can buck and spook if the weather changes. Anytime a horse or pony has had several days of rest, be on guard. If he is too fresh, just longe him a few minutes instead of letting him dump you. Don't let other riders deter you from your plan to longe a fresh pony with their accusations of "chicken." "Better a live chicken than a hurt or dead duck."

Another important function of the longe line is that it enables you to practice your position and to develop your ability to be "tight" on the horse. Sometimes your teacher will give you a "longe line lesson," a necessary but always dreaded affair, as it is hard to ride without reins and/or stirrups. In our barn the riders often take turns longeing (and teaching) each other.

First make sure the horse or pony is quiet enough. If in doubt, it is always safest to start a rider on the longe line with both reins and stirrups. Then remove the stirrups. After a while the rider can practice without reins and stirrups both. Besides the usual walk, trot (sitting and posting), and canter, there are several good exercises to practice as the rider gets more secure. (The photographs on pages 82–87 illustrate some favorite exercises.) Eventually a small jump can be included. Begin with just a rail on the ground. Set it perpendicular to a fence line so the horse cannot run out on the far side. Again, start jumping with reins and stirrups and then remove them when the rider is getting tight enough to jump without them.

Working without stirrups on the flat, over fences and especially on the longe line is the best exercise for strength-

Some exercises to practice on the longe line. After starting with reins and stirrups, both are removed and Cullen grasps pommel (front) of the saddle with her inside hand and cantle (back) of the saddle with her outside hand. This exercise is the most secure once reins and stirrups are gone; therefore it should be the first. Walk, trot and canter can be practiced. This exercise is a good one for following the horse's movement with your seat.

Once she feels comfortable without reins and stirrups, she puts her hands on her hips, or she can slip one behind her back and let the other hang down.

Next she slowly spreads her arms like a bird. (It is important to do this slowly so as not to startle the horse and be dumped off his rear end!) Once her arms are outstretched, she practices turning toward the inside and then the outside of the circle. As she gets better at it, she practices this at the trot and the canter. Another related exercise is to rotate the arms front to back—at all gaits—again slowly at first, not to scare the horse.

As the handler holds the pony, first Cullen lies on his neck, then touches her toes with the opposite hand, and finally lies on his back, being careful not to lose her leg position each time as she sits up. Someone should *always* hold the pony for these exercises.

After a strenuous lesson sometimes a relaxed bareback ride is in order. Here Frosty wears his halter and two lead ropes, instead of a bridle. (This is only recommended for very quiet ponies.)

Finally Frosty convinces her that he would really like to have a few mouthfuls of grass.

Here a more formal bareback ride is planned. Frosty wears a pelham bridle and Cullen holds the two reins correctly. Riding bareback helps riders develop "feel."

ening your legs and developing a secure seat. Ride without stirrups as often as possible, always being careful that the horse is quiet enough.

After a few weeks or months you will start to feel more and more that you and your horse are partners, a team of two. This feeling of togetherness is what makes riding horses different from all other sports. From the very beginning you want to develop the habit of gaining rapport with your horse. Try to understand both his frame of mind and his point of view. Then figure out how to persuade him, or coerce him if necessary, to do what you want him to do. Be firm, but not rough, as you coax him to do what you want him to do. Close attention to flatwork is the foundation for good riding, whether for pleasure or for competition. Diligent flatwork is also the foundation for the horse's obedience to the rider's aids.

Chapter 3

Riding Over Jumps

ONCE YOU FEEL pretty secure at the trot and canter, it is time to start a little jumping. My feeling is that knowing diagonals and leads is not totally necessary at this stage. Your teacher may not agree on this point, and you should always abide by his or her program. Trust your teacher's judgment. Nothing is more annoying than hearing "But so-and-so said . . ." My response is always that the trainer who is responsible for your progress and your safety should always be the ultimate authority. Go ride with "so-and-so" if you really think it is better at that barn.

Starting Over Jumps

The Half-Seat

Before actually starting to jump fences, you should be able to hold the half-seat at the trot and canter. The half-seat, or two-point position, is also called the jumping position. It is an excellent exercise for strengthening your legs and deepening your heels even if you have no intention of ever jumping.

Here is what to do: First shorten your reins and rise so that your seat does not touch the saddle. Your upper body should be inclined slightly forward. Your weight should rest totally in your heels, which you press down to absorb the shock of the horse's movement and/or jump.

If I were to choose one exercise to improve a rider's position and strength, the half-seat at all gaits is the one. Practice it continually especially in your beginning years of riding.

The Release

Finally, when jumping lessons are in order, the rider usually starts with trotting between specific standards and trotting over rails on the ground. The most important thing to practice at this point is the release, so that when the horse jumps, he has the freedom to use his head and neck properly. When you are starting out, the best plan is to reach up and grab a piece of mane to make sure the thrust of the jump does not unseat you or cause you to fall back and bang

Trotting over a rail on the ground. She is not posting but holding her half-seat, also known as the jumping position, or "two-point."

Practicing the half-seat is an excellent exercise for strengthening your legs and developing a secure position. Here Cullen demonstrates the half-seat at the trot and the canter. All her weight is in her heels and her seat is just out of the saddle.

Cantering over a rail on the ground. Riders just starting to jump should practice the "crest release," which means you rest your hands on the crest or top of the horse's neck when going over the top of the rail or jump. Cantering over rails on the ground is the best way to simulate jumping jumps, for everything but the flight of the jump can be practiced: the half-seat, the approach, the release, the departure. Notice that her lower leg has slipped and her toes point out too much.

The first crossrail—very correct and lovely for a beginner. Her release is a little exaggerated and her lower leg has slipped a bit, but her eyes are up and basically her position is just fine.

Here we see more "polish." Her heels are down and there is a straight line from the pony's mouth to her hand.

Incorrect: Here she is "climbing up his neck," her body is way ahead of him and her leg has slipped back.

Correct: She approaches the jump in her half-seat.

Incorrect: She is sitting behind the motion and driving with her seat. This driving position is absolutely necessary if one is riding a stopper, but for a novice rider it is not appropriate.

Correct: She is holding her half-seat on landing, but her heel has slipped up a bit. She needs to sink into her heels as they land over the jump. Her upper body is just right, not ahead of or behind her mount. She supports herself well with her hands on the pony's neck.

Incorrect: Here she is standing too erect and is over the pommel of the saddle. She needs to drop into her heels more.

Correct: Approaching the jump in good balance.

Incorrect: The rider is too erect here and the pony's stride is too long and strung out.

She is ducking off to the right instead of looking between his ears toward the next jump. Also her lower leg has slipped back somewhat. Again sinking into her heels would correct the situation.

Here her position is quite good and she is using the crest release.
Beginning jumping riders need to learn this release to support
themselves without hurting the horse's mouth. Her eyes are
directed straight ahead. Her lower leg has slipped back just a bit,
but her heel is down. She is "in the middle" of her pony, neither
ahead nor behind; just where she should be.

Over this jump she is demonstrating a nice deep heel. As soon as her seat is more secure we will work on a straight line from her elbow to the pony's mouth. For now the crest release is fine, although somewhat exaggerated here.

Good, correct form—pony and rider. Her eyes are up, her weight is in her heels, her crest release is almost becoming a "following hand" here, she is "in the middle" of her pony, neither ahead of him nor behind him.

him in the mouth. So while approaching the rail (and later the jump) in the half-seat, feel his mouth through the reins and rest your hands firmly up on his neck to support yourself, or if necessary grab some mane. Once you have mastered the release trotting over a single rail, you can do a line of two rails at least 60 feet apart, first at the trot and then at the canter. Then practice: Feel his mouth, release. Feel, release. Feel . . .

Usually the next step after trotting and cantering rails on the ground is to start trotting small crossrails: first a single X, then a line, and finally a little pattern or course. (See the diagrams on pages 66–69 for some very basic patterns and courses.) Your teacher will know when you are ready to canter to the jumps and finally to jump a little higher. Some trainers encourage riders to practice cantering rails and low jumps between lessons. Others prefer their students to jump only under supervision. Here again you must respect your teacher's judgment.

When You Land

When you land over the jump it is important to know what you will do next. You have many options. One is "to stop on a line," that is, halt promptly, smoothly and straight, facing directly away from the rail or jump. A second option is to turn left or right afterwards and then halt. Another plan is to circle left or right and then halt. Any of these plans is appropriate, but be sure you always have a plan. Later, when you are jumping courses and the fences are coming up quickly, you will be glad you developed the habit of planning when you land over a jump. I still suffer from not developing that habit early on. Sometimes I slip my gears and forget to organize when my horse lands!

The Importance of Good Flatwork

You will soon notice the tremendous value of good flatwork as you begin your jumping career. Riders and horses both must have a sound background in flatwork if they intend to become competent over jumps.

For instance, as mentioned earlier, nowadays in the show ring, flying changes are absolutely necessary even in short-stirrup crossrail classes if you want to be at the top of the class, not the bottom. Many horses do them almost automatically, but since some do not, you need to know exactly how to balance a horse so he can execute the flying change properly.

Seeing the Distance: Balance, Rhythm and Track

Many people get very hung up on "seeing a distance." Certainly some riders do "find the jumps" more easily than others, but the main reason they do "see the jumps" is that they have an instinctive understanding of their horse's balance and rhythm as well as a keen awareness of the good track to the jump. If the balance, rhythm and track are correct, the jump will be at least decent, if not wonderful.

Young riders must learn to tune in to their horse's balance. Is he on his forehand? Does he drift to the left or right? He needs to be straight and jump the middle of the fence. The rhythm is easier to understand and regulate. It is more than just fast and slow. It is often a matter of RPM rather than MPH. The horse's stride needs to be lively, but not too long or too short. As one good old horseman once explained to me, "As you go around a course, try to keep him at 35, then you can go up to 40 or down to 30 without major adjustments. If you go at 30, to get him up to 40 will be a project. So will getting him from 40 quickly back to 30." The numbers are not as important as the concept: Go medium and then you can move up or down as needed.

Of the three important elements—balance, rhythm and track—the easiest to make correct is the track itself. As you come around the corner of the ring to the jump, make sure the horse does not cut the turn or do the opposite— drift out on the turn. In other words he should not fall in or fall out, but follow the arc of the circle around to the jump. If you heeded Frosty Lad's introductory remarks, you will know without even thinking that much of track savvy depends on remembering where the ingate is. Every horse at least thinks about falling out toward the ingate as he goes past and falling in on the far end of the ring. Some horses just think about it, but most do it! If you forget where the ingate is, you will definitely have trouble figuring out how to ride the track.

The most important rule for those who do not "see the distance" is to be patient and wait until you do. Don't grab at the distance you "think" you see, for you will alarm your horse with last-minute spurring. Nor should you break up his stride with rough hands grabbing at his mouth. Wait it out. The jump is not going anywhere, and you will get to it eventually, so just be patient. Sit still, keep your hands still and let the horse jump when he gets to it.

If you have developed the habit of organizing when you land over a jump and go into the turn, then as you come out of the turn you can relax and "let go" and allow the horse to show you the distance. (Related distances between the jumps will be dealt with later.) Easy to say, but not all that easy to do. Years of practice will probably help!

Schooling Over Low Jumps

Trotting fences discourages anticipation by horse and rider. The rider may hold the half-seat as he trots the fence or may post the trot, sitting only the last couple of strides. With horses that need a lot of leg to hold them together, it may be better if the rider sits the trot all the way to the jump. I start nearly all sessions with trotting low fences.

Basic Exercises

Departures from the fence are as important as approaches, so upon landing you should incorporate one of the three following exercises:

1. Stop on a line. Then turn on forehand. Concentrate on straightness.

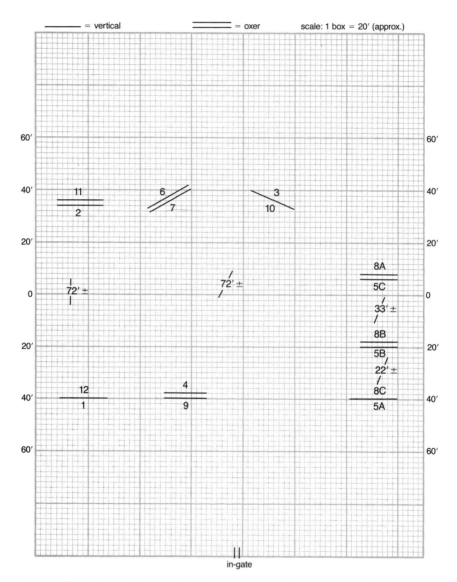

Basic Schooling Course for Young Riders. *Note to course builders:* All these jumps should be constructed so they can be jumped from either direction for maximum use of the pattern.

2. Shift hands to the outside, press the horse out toward the rail with your inside leg as you bend him around that leg. Halt at the end of the ring, or make a circle before halting. Halt if he is very strong. Circle if he needs minor organizing.

3. Shift hands to the outside, ask for a flying change if necessary, continue around the turn holding out and looking in toward the next jump. Halt at the jump.

Practice holding the half-seat—between jumps as well as over the jumps. An especially effective exercise is to hold the half-seat through a series of gymnastics.

Alternate trotting and cantering fences with halts, turns, and lines after the jump to reinforce the horse's obedience to your aids.

When schooling, see that the horse remains ridable and obedient between jumps. If he gets above his pace or misses a change of lead, circle him. If he then gets strong after the change, circle again until he settles.

Circling is a wonderful settling device before and after the jump. With a sensitive horse especially, circling works better than pulling him up abruptly when he gets above his pace. That may rattle him.

More Exercises

An elaborate course is not necessary for practicing simple exercises over jumps. Any of the jumps in the diagram (see page 108) can be jumped individually. A rider with horse sense usually begins with trotting and then cantering the simplest single fences, jumping them toward the ingate, "home," the first time. Remember Frosty's remarks in his Introduction about understanding the horse's point of view and trying to "think like a horse."

After a few simple jumps, the gymnastic on the right side of the ring is a good exercise. Start with it very low—crossrails even—and jump it both directions at the canter. Gradually make it higher and wider: 2' or 2'6" for ponies, 3' or 3'3" high and wide at the most for horses. After mastering the gymnastic, add fences 6 and 2, and perhaps finally the line 3 and 4.

When you ride a line like the line of fences 1 and 2, for example, in the diagram, your horse will canter a certain number of strides between those two jumps. The distance between those jumps will be somewhere near a multiple of 12 feet. Courses for novice riders are usually set on the 12-foot stride. Allowing 6 feet for landing and 6 feet for takeoff, if the distance is 72 feet then your horse will canter 5 strides between those two jumps. Most ponies will canter 6 strides. Whether the 5 strides will be forward or steady depends on the horse's natural length of stride and/or his temperament. The 5 strides will be forward for a lazy and/or short-strided horse. That means when you land over fence 1 you need to close your legs and urge him forward to fence 2. If your horse has a long stride and/or a keen temperament, the 5 will be right there, so just keep cantering but don't hurry. If you jump the line backwards, in over the oxer (fence 11), then for a keen and/or long-strided horse the 5 to fence 12 will be easy. You will have to slow him down. The oxer will carry him farther into the line than a vertical will and you are going toward "home," so you will get there much easier.

As you know, you have to understand the horse's point of view. It is often a matter of common sense. The same 5-stride distance rides differently, depending on when it occurs in the course. For most horses, 72 feet will be a bit continuing if it is the first line of the course, but if it is the last line of the course it will ride short for most. When it comes to riding courses well, it is not just a matter of talent and "feel." That all helps, but using your brain is at least as important if not more important than talent, skill and a fancy horse.

Once you have mastered riding the 5 strides back and forth, then an exercise in stride control is in order. Practice adding a stride. In a slow collected canter, jump into the line and fit in 6 strides in the 72-foot line. Again you will find the exercise easier going away from "home," the in-gate, and jumping in over a vertical, so practice that first. Next work on jumping in over the oxer and making sure you add the extra stride early, not at the last minute in front of the vertical. Once you master fitting in the 6 strides going both directions, practice alternating 5 and 6 strides: 5 up and 6 back then 6 up and 5 back. S-turns on the ends are useful for turning yourself around.

The line of fences 3 and 4 is called a broken line. As you come around the corner, if you want to go directly from 3 to 4, you must "look for your line," that is, look for fence 4 beyond fence 3. When you see fence 4 between the standards of 3 you have your line, then look for a distance to 3. Always seek your line first and then the distance. Then look for your distance to 3 and continue directly to 4 in 5 strides. If you want to do an indirect line from 3 to 4, jump separately as it is built and ride straight 3 strides, turn a bit left and ride 3 more strides. That is also called a broken line. Practice doing the direct 5 strides and the indirect 6. Both are correct, and you should be comfortable doing both options.

Once you have mastered the 3 to 4 line, work back and forth over 6 and 4. Again, if you are doing a direct line, you need to line up the second jump as you come around the turn to the first. Jump across the first jump into the line and across the second jump as well. Also practice the indirect line between 6 and 4. Jump each fence as it is built and add a stride.

The 6/7 jump alone poses several interesting possibilities. Cantering up the length of the ring away from the ingate, be sure you ride right up to the 6/7 jump. Horses back off of jumps alone at the far end of the ring away from the in-gate. Jumping it the other way on the left lead enables you to practice jumping off a short turn. Jumping it the other way on the right lead, you can practice looking early around the 2 jump to find your distance on a really short, awkward turn.

To do what I call the serpentine exercise, cut the ring in half and jump in the pattern of fences 11, 7, 3, 5C. Jump, turn, jump, turn, jump, turn, jump. There is little space in this exercise, so you must be sure to use all the area that is available to you. Do not let your horse anticipate and cut in to the jump as you round the turn. Stay on the track and keep your rhythm/pace. Short, tight turns will cause your horse to slow down, so make sure he keeps going enough, but at the same time do not rush the turn.

Even in a ring where the course is very simple and straightforward, like this one, countless options exist. The best way to become a good rider is to experiment with the possible options. The jumps need not ever be high for beginner and intermediate riders; a maximum of 3' or 3'3" is plenty, and for most 2' is enough. Regardless of the height of the fences, the exercises, the "problems," and the questions asked are essentially the same. Master them at 2' or 3' and you will someday find 4' or 5' courses easy.

This simple diagram offers numerous possibilities for lessons and for dozens of patterns to practice.

Riders and trainers alike must remember not to "use up" their horses in their zeal to become more proficient. There is an old saying among good horsemen that for every fence a horse jumps, there is one less at the end. Don't just cruise around mindlessly over fences. Make every jump count. A viable compromise for riders yearning to improve with horses that do not need to jump 1,000 jumps is to work over rails on the ground in various patterns and to hop over patterns of very low jumps. Everything is the same with a rail on the ground or a low jump except the actual flight over a large jump, so lines, angles and turns can be mastered without using up and abusing the horse. Landing over larger jumps takes its toll on any horse's legs.

Once you are cantering around low (2' or 3') courses, you are getting close to being ready to go horse showing. Again, rely on your teacher to decide when and where you

More bareback riding—good for developing a tight seat. The pony has his bridle on, a clear indication that something more than a casual walk is planned. Cullen's legs and hands are very correct. I would like her back to be straighter, however.

She found a little jump to pop over. All this bareback work is fun and makes for a better rider at the same time.

will make your debut. If you are young enough to show in the Short Stirrup division, that may be where to start. Older riders can start in Maiden and Novice Equitation and/or Children's Hunters.

Meanwhile, keep working on your basics at home. You will find you enjoy riding more and more as you become more experienced. The more you learn, the more you will find that you need to learn. One activity that develops basics is riding bareback. Be sure your teacher approves. Riding bareback unsupervised can be dangerous, so make sure you have the go-ahead before you discard your saddle. Riding bareback makes you tighter. You will develop muscles to hold yourself on the horse, and you will develop more "feel." It is easier to feel what your horse is doing when there is no saddle between you and him. The third and most important reason to ride bareback is that it is fun!

Chapter 4

Starting to Horse Show

ONCE YOUR TRAINER has decided that you have progressed to the point where you are ready to compete in a horse show, you have to do a lot to get yourself prepared for the big day. Count on him or her to select the appropriate horse show and the classes in the show that will suit you best.

Preparations Before Horse Show Day

If you are riding a school horse, the stable will probably bring all the necessary tack and equipment. Even so, there is no harm in politely checking to see that everything you will need is packed. Check with your teacher to find out exactly where the show is and what time you should be there. You will certainly want to make sure your clothes are all clean and your boots are polished. Don't wait till the day before the show to check your clothes. Your parents won't appreciate doing ten errands at the last minute, so get everything together a few days ahead of time. This is not a bad habit to get into early in your riding career. Also be sure you have directions to the show so you don't waste precious time getting lost.

Clothes and Equipment

A young rider looks well turned out in jodhpurs and jodhpur boots or laced paddock boots. Buff and rust are the usual colors for jodhpurs. Both look fine, although buff will show dirt sooner than rust. Later, when you are past the pony and limit equitation divisions and are showing in open equitation, hunter or jumper classes, it's time to wear breeches and boots. Ready-made stretch breeches usually fit well and last a long time if they are properly cared for. They should be washed in cold water and line dried or sent to the cleaners. (A clothes dryer will ruin the strapping (leather patches) on the knees of your pants.)

Boots will probably be your most expensive item of clothing. For the best appearance and fit, invest in a pair of custom-made boots, either black dress boots or laced field boots. Have them made unlined. Unlined boots will be softer and therefore more comfortable and will allow a better feel of the horse. They will prove their worth in the long run over most ready-made boots, which often are too stiff,

Neatly braided pigtails are cute for young girls still wearing jodhpurs. When they graduate from the pony ranks, it's time for breeches and tall boots. Also it is time to put the hair up under the hunt cap.

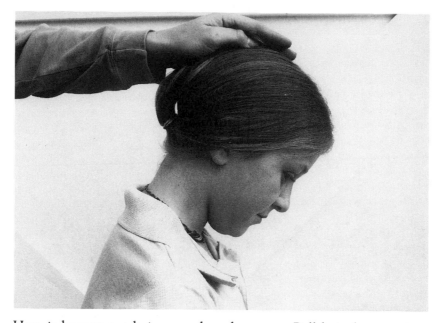

Here is how to put hair up under a hunt cap: Pull hair down over the ears to a very low pony tail in the back. Fasten it securely with an elastic or a hair clip. Wispy hair may need bobby pins behind the ears to keep it organized. Flip the ends up and fasten neatly with a hair clip or bobby pins. Then put on the hair net. Tie a knot in it if it is too big (it usually is), and finally slip the hat on carefully from back to front, tucking in loose ends. Don't wait till the horse show to get your hair up the first time. Practice at home until you have it down pat. If you want to look poised and polished at your first horse show and every one thereafter, tidy hair is a key factor.

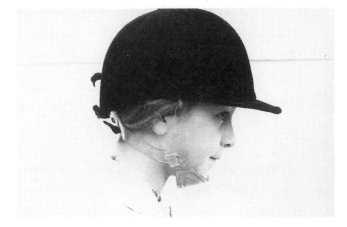

too short or too wide in the leg. A careful shopper may find some decent ready-made boots or secondhand (outgrown) boots that are comfortable and fit well.

You will look your best in neat, unobtrusive riding clothes. Of course, nothing fits quite so well as custom-made shirts and jackets, but most riders can get nearly the same effect by having a ready-made coat altered to fit. A plain navy blue or dark green coat with dark buttons is a good choice. Avoid loud colors and bright plaids, yet on the other hand, a formal black coat is a bit severe for young riders just starting to show.

Girl's ratcatcher shirts or chokers should be in solid pastel colors or white. A choker or shirt collar must fit perfectly. Anything large or baggy looks very sloppy indeed. A few well-placed stitches on a big collar and choker can make all the difference. Many girls now put their monograms (initials) on their chokers in colors that coordinate with their jackets. This is a nice touch. Boys should wear their conservative ties neatly tacked down, not flapping in the wind.

As for headgear, a black harness hat (approved by the American Horse Shows Association) is correct for any occasion. Girls with long hair should keep it pinned up securely under a hair net. Braids are cute on a young girl up to about the age of ten or twelve. Boys should keep their hair short enough for a neat appearance. Wear the absolute minimum of jewelry.

Gloves are a matter of taste and personal preference. If you wear them, they should be dark brown. I think there is just as good a feel with gloves on as without them, and

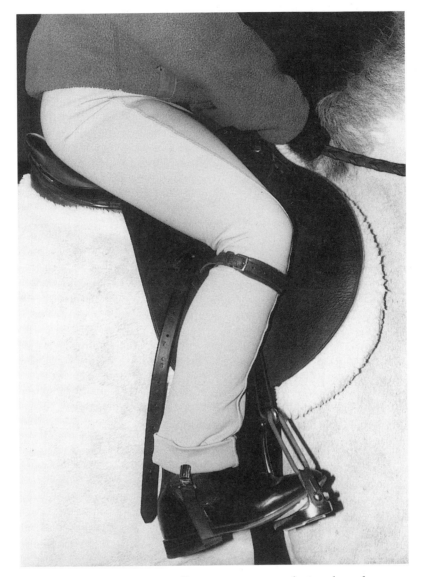

This rider has the correct jodhpur straps properly in place for competing in a horse show. The leather strap under her knee is buckled with the strap end facing toward the rear of the pony. The elastic strap clamps to her jodhpurs and goes on the outside of her boots. These straps keep the jodhpurs in place. Without them, the pants ride up and twist.

they give you a more polished look in equitation classes. In rainy weather they are essential because the reins get very slippery.

Whether or not you wear spurs depends on your expertise as a rider, on your horse's disposition and on the situation at hand. If you wear spurs before you have achieved good control of your seat, hands and lower leg, there is a risk of getting into trouble, since an unintentional jab can turn the quietest plug into a runaway. Spurs are more often needed in hot weather than in cold and in small, spooky indoor rings than in open fields. Still, some horses are so sluggish that they need prodding, even in the biggest field on the coldest, windiest day. You must rely on your trainer's judgment, and use your own judgment as well, when deciding whether or not to wear spurs.

I prefer Prince of Wales spurs to the hammerhead type. To me, they look more graceful and elegant. They come in lengths from ½ inch to 1½ inches, so you can buy exactly the length that suits your needs. Most riders find eventually that they need a variety of spurs of different lengths to be able to deal with all situations.

A stick, I believe, is a necessary aid for every rider who is past the beginning stage. Almost any horse can learn to accept the stick, no matter how tense and nervous he may be, and by using it you can often prevent a serious situation from developing. Learn to carry the stick in either hand comfortably. In most cases, it should be used behind the saddle, but occasionally a tap on the shoulder is useful— for example, when a horse is about to pop his shoulder out on a turn. Sticks come in a variety of lengths. A 14-inch stick is about right. It is long enough to be effective but short enough to be held easily and out of the horse's range of vision. Informal and unrecognized (by the AHSA) shows usually require only that young riders have the proper helmet, boots and jodhpurs. A proper riding jacket and riding shirt are not always necessary at these horse shows. Check to be sure, though.

Horse Show Check List

HORSE
Saddle
Saddle pads (fleece or foam)
Baby pad (to wear under saddle pad while schooling)
Girth
Martingale and/or breastplate
Bridle(s)
Extra bits if necessary

Grooming box (see photograph on page 6)
One or two pails
Hay net/extra bale of hay
Grain if needed

Blankets
Sheet
Rainsheet
Coolers

RIDER
Hat
Hair net, clips and bobby pins for the girls
Shirt and tie or choker
Jodhpurs or breeches
Boots (polished)
Spurs
Stick
Gloves
(all clean and in good condition)

Because weather can change, always bring:
Raincoat
Warm parka
Rubbers
A small bag for all extras

Last but not least:
Directions to the horse show.

Divisions at Horse Shows

Let's talk about the divisions that are available at most local horse shows. Leadline and Walk-Trot are self-explanatory. In some leadline classes riders are asked to trot, so in those classes knowing how to post is key. Walk-trot equitation riders are of course expected to know how to post and to be on the correct diagonal.

The Short Stirrup division is usually open to riders under

Cullen and her mother have arrived at the horse show and Mom is checking to make sure the hat is on properly.

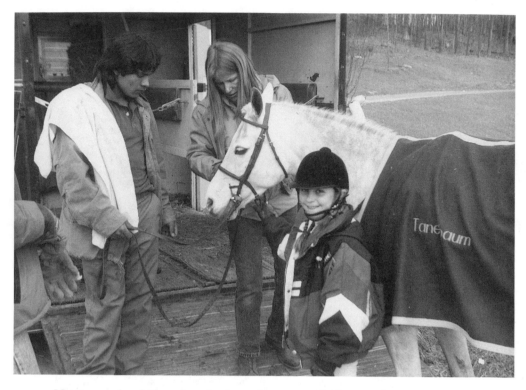

Having unloaded and tacked up the pony, Cullen is almost ready to get on and school in the ring.

Other riders are tacking up their ponies, preparing for the first class of the day.

The riders are gathering in the schooling area. A practice jump is on the left.

This young rider is carrying her saddle properly. Notice that she is wearing correctly fitting tall boots.

This is the main show ring. Riders are permitted to work their horses on the flat, but no schooling is permitted over fences. Rules vary from show to show. Small local shows usually permit schooling over the jump. The big "A" shows seldom do. Competitors must understand and conform to schooling rules.

On her way to the ring, Cullen gives a little boy a chance to see how he likes riding.

Here Cullen is competing with her new pony. He is a very good jumper, as you can see. Cullen's position is correct, although the pony's big effort over this big fence jumped her a little loose.

twelve years or sometimes under ten. Classes in this division are on the flat and over tiny jumps, and even crossrails are offered. Sometimes the horse is judged and sometimes the rider's equitation is judged. Read the specs in the prize list so you know the judge's focus. If you get in the habit of doing this, it can save you a lot of grief later on.

Once a rider has progressed beyond Short Stirrup, there are numerous Equitation classes, starting with Maiden on the Flat (walk, trot and canter) and Over Fences of 2'. Maiden Equitation classes are for riders who have never won a blue ribbon (first prize) in an AHSA-rated horse show; novice, for riders who have not won three blue ribbons; limit, six blues, etc. Children's Hunter classes are for ponies and horses to be judged on their style of jumping over low jumps 2' to 2'9" for ponies, 3' for horses.

The Pony Hunter division offers three sections: Small, 12.2 hands and under; Medium, 13.2 hands and under; and Large, 14.2 hands and under. Horses and ponies are measured by "hands." One hand equals 4 inches. Simple arithmetic tells us that smalls may not exceed 50 inches; mediums, 54 inches; and larges, 58 inches.

Every pony and horse shown by a junior must be measured by two officials from the AHSA at its first AHSA-recognized horse show. The pony receives a temporary card at that point, stating its height, and later a "current measurement card." Any pony's height may be questioned anytime, so riders must be sure to bring the card to every AHSA-recognized horse show. Ponies that show in the Pony Hunter division, especially at the "A" horse shows' competitive events, are traditionally fancier than those in the Children's Hunter Pony division. By "fancier," I mean prettier to look at, and their way of going and style of jumping are often superior. Some of the best teaching ponies, including Frosty Lad, are traditionally shown in the Children's Hunter Pony division. That division is perfect for low intermediate riders. Actually, Frosty Lad himself has been known to jump up and win a good Small Pony Hunter class now and then, especially if it is the first class in a spooky ring. That's part of the fun of horse showing. You never know who will be the winner at the end of the class. Certain ponies are more competitive than others, but on a given day anything can happen!

The next step from the Children's Hunter division and the Pony Hunter division are the Mini Medal and Mini Maclay classes, where the rider's seat and control are judged over a course of 3'3" jumps. Usually the courses are very similar and often exactly the same as the big Hunter Seat Equitation classes: the AHSA Medal and the ASPCA Maclay. Riders compete in those classes at local AHSA-recognized shows as well as at the "A," "B" and "C"-rated events. The "big" equitation events—the PHA, the AS-PCA Maclay, the AHSA Medal, the USET and the Capitol Cup—are beyond the scope of this book, and I recommend you read George Morris's book, *Hunter Seat Equitation* (Doubleday, 1990), the classic in the field.

The Day of the Horse Show:
Early Morning Preparations

Finally the day of your first horse show arrives. Allow plenty of time to get up, get dressed and get to the show. Be sure you have directions to the show. If you care for and transport the horse yourself, have everything in order and packed the night before, so there are no delays in the morning. When you get to the show, check in with your teacher for further information. You will probably ride around the grounds, work your horse on the flat and even over some fences. Some shows permit schooling in the ring, and you may want to ride in the ring on the flat and possibly over the fences as well if schooling is permitted. If the ring is crowded, do not let the crowds distract you or rattle you. Just calmly tune in to your trainer and go on with your plan and finish up when the call to clear the ring is heard.

Classes on the Flat

Equitation

The Hunter Seat Equitation judge will compare the basic position of the riders—seat, legs and hands—as well as their control over the horses or ponies. He or she also will be judging the riders' influence on their mounts. The horses or ponies should be well balanced, straight on the long sides of the ring and nicely bent around the ends.

Show what you know about riding on the flat. Before the class starts, do a few transitions to catch the judge's eye. When the judge calls for the class to reverse, instead of just turning around, demonstrate a turn on the forehand. A horse show is just that. You should show off how good you are and hide your faults. For instance, if you bounce around at the sitting trot, trot your horse very slowly, so he doesn't bounce you much, and hide behind another horse if possible.

Inexperienced show riders usually rush to obey the judge's commands. Be as prompt as possible but not at the cost of getting the wrong lead. When there is a call to canter, position your horse by squeezing him with your outside leg behind the girth. This prepares him to canter on the proper lead before you actually ask for the canter.

In flat classes you will want to make sure the judge sees you. Check out where he is sitting or standing. Try to stay by yourself as much as possible so he can really watch you ride. Sometimes as trainer I have difficulty finding my riders in the ring. How can those who hide expect the judges to find them? The first trot is especially important because that is when most judges pick up the entries they want to use in the final lineup. If the judge misses you at the first trot, the most you can hope for is a low ribbon. In your zeal to be seen by the judge, make sure you are not rude to your fellow competitors. Try not to cut them off or, worse yet, bump into them. Before entering the ring make sure you know if the flat class is an Equitation class or a Hunter Under Saddle class. In the former, the rider is judged; in the latter, the horse. Traditionally, in Equitation classes the rider shows his horse with a somewhat shorter rein than he would in an Under Saddle class.

The procedure for flat classes is usually (but not always) as follows, so listen carefully in case the judge varies his commands: When all competitors have gathered in the ring, the command will be to walk. Find a place by yourself so the judge can see you on the first trot. After the trot he will probably call for a walk and then the canter. Then you will reverse and repeat that pattern. When he has made his decision, you will be told to line up. Trot right in and line up in the center, so your number is right in front of him, in hopes that he will want to double-check your number and give you a ribbon: blue for first; red, second; yellow, third; white, fourth; pink, fifth; green, sixth; purple, seventh; or brown, eighth. Any ribbon is a good ribbon.

Hunter Under Saddle

Hunter Under Saddle classes are also judged on the flat, but in these classes the horse or pony is being judged. "Light contact with the horse's or pony's mouth is required" is recommended in the AHSA rule book. Manners and way of moving are compared. The horse or pony should be quiet and obedient, but not dull. He should prick his ears and seem happy and alert. A sour expression and ears pinned back will be penalized. He should be well balanced and move close to the ground with a long slow sweeping stride at the trot and at the canter. If he has a good trot and canters with a high stride, show off at the trot and hide at the canter, and vice versa. Show his good points and hide his faults.

Classes Over Fences

For the classes over fences, be sure that you know the course and try to watch as much as possible before you mount up. Review the course plan with your teacher and walk the course if that is permitted. The jumping order and a diagram of the course will be posted at the ingate. As you study the course, make sure if there is a dotted line, you know where it is. A dotted line across the ring on the diagram means that anyone who crosses that line while making his circle will automatically be eliminated. Dotted lines are great time savers and must be observed even in Short Stirrup classes. Once you are on the horse, you will want to concentrate on getting him ready, not wondering what the course is.

Allow five to ten horses in front of you in planning the warm-up time. For the first class you may need the extra time of ten horses. After that, five should be enough because you will not need to do as much. You do not want to be ready too early and stand around a long time before you go in. Being rushed at the last minute is hectic and equally inappropriate. It's important to develop a sense of time, so you give yourself enough but not too much time. You should also take into consideration your mount's temperament. Placid horses do better if they go right in the ring after schooling. High-strung or nervous ones need a few minutes to settle after schooling before they compete. If you do have to wait around on a placid horse, smack him with your stick or give him a good kick before you enter the ring. Make sure he is awake. However, if you are rushed at the last minute with a high-strung horse, go directly to the ingate when called. Once in the ring, walk a few steps and soothe him with your voice before picking up the canter and start-ing your round.

Riding the Course

Whether the class is a Short Stirrup Crossrail class or the Olympic Games, once in the ring, rider and mount must concentrate on the job at hand. Some riders are less easily distracted and therefore more able than others to remember their plan. To some extent concentration is a learned skill and one that riders need to develop from the very beginning. Reviewing the course several times in your mind before going in the ring will help you concentrate while actually in the ring.

The opening circle establishes the pace for the course. A sluggish horse needs to get above his pace early in the circle and then settle into it, so he is not behind the eight ball at the first fence. An eager horse, however, will build as he goes around the course, so the rider must be sure to slow him down on the ends of the ring, or he will be way ahead of himself by the end of the course.

As Frosty Lad reminds us in his Introduction, the good rider must be "tuned in" to his or her horse or pony. While analyzing the course, scope it out from your mount's point of view. Some show rings are impressive and some are spooky, just as some horses are easily impressed and some are quite spooky. "Know your horse as you analyze the course" should be the motto of any serious rider. Beyond the general look of the ring, figure out which lines, angles and turns might pose problems as well as which jumps look impressive or spooky. A general rule of thumb should be: "Be ready to override the difficult parts and be careful not to override the simpler parts."

Riders just starting their show careers should remember that at first they will need to rely on mounts that "show them where the jumps are"—old troopers who know their way around the ring. The "cute puke" will never teach you to ride or make you a winner. Instead, he will have you soon searching around for another sport.

If you do not win a lot in the beginning, keep honing your skills and eventually you may be able to graduate to a fancier mount. Perhaps the most important attribute for a rider to have is perseverance. The willingness to keep on trying is a quality to be more valued than talent, the right build, wealth or anything else. Learning to ride is not easy, and winning in competition does not usually happen right away.

Remember when you ride into the ring, you are in a horse show. You must show you are the best. The ring is yours for the next minute or two, so make the most of it. For some this attitude comes naturally. Others have to work to develop it. Believe me, it is well worth developing.

Hunter Classes: Patterns

Pony Hunter and Children's Hunter courses are usually quite simple and straightforward. Usually there are eight jumps: side, diagonal, side, diagonal or a variation of that. Hunters are judged on "performance, manners, style of jumping, and way of going." Performance is the horse's evenness and smoothness as he proceeds around the course: over the fences, between the fences and around the turns. Hunters should snatch their knees up and round their backs, so when the performances of several horses are about the same, the style of jumping should determine which will be the winner. As in the under saddle classes, "the way of going" also is either a plus or a minus. When I am judging, the manners of a child's mount are particularly important. Another often overlooked important factor is suitability. Size as well as temperament should be considered. The only picture worse than a huge child on a tiny pony is a tiny child overmounted on a huge horse.

Equitation Classes

In equitation classes the rider is being judged, but of course the overall picture is what makes the difference. A horse and rider combination that seems to fit together will excel over the odd-looking pair if the performances, that is, their execution of the course, are equivalent.

From the opening circle, the rider's basic position and control are being judged as well as the actual execution of the course. Accuracy is of utmost importance. The rider must "nail" the eight or however many jumps there are. Particularly at the lower levels of Hunter Seat Equitation (maiden, novice, and even limit classes) the rider's position is carefully scrutinized, for in the early stages most riders have not developed a style of their own. At that level— and really at all levels—the basics are what count. If you have applied what you have learned in your lessons and in this book, you should be able to demonstrate sound basics in the show ring.

After the Class

When you have finished your round, whether it was good, bad, or mediocre, analyze your performance. Review the entire course slowly and carefully in your mind, figuring out which parts were good and which were not so good. Then try to figure out why. Probably your round was not perfect; probably it was not totally horrible either. Be realistic and objective as you sort out your thoughts, much easier said than done. This is a skill we all must learn to develop. If you have a trainer or ground person helping you, review your performance with him or her as well. You will find over the years that plain old common sense will always stand you in good stead when you review your courses.

A young rider who keeps her green horse at home and comes to my barn for the occasional lesson complained to me one day that her horse was stopping all the time at the shows. At home and during her lessons, we had the opposite problem; he hurried to the jumps. To correct his rushing, she often circled in front of the jumps until he settled. Common sense helped us find the solution. Obviously, the green horse found the unfamiliar ring impressive and the jumps scary. For the first time in his life he needed to be "ridden up to the jump." In other words, the young rider had to kick him to get him up to the jumps, a new experience for her as well.

At the next show she rode up to the jumps and he never even thought of stopping. At that show the rider learned firsthand that a horse's resistances come in pairs. When she kicked him to the jumps, he would bolt away upon landing. She had to be ready for the second resistance and slow him down immediately upon landing. Likewise you will find that you will learn a lot at horse shows; you will soon discover your own and your mount's weaknesses and strengths. The thinking rider will be able to turn those weaknesses into strengths. No matter how bad a show you have, you will always gain something from it. Sometimes things have to get worse before they get better. Make yourself think positively even if you do not have a good day.

Appendix

Activities Available to Young Riders

T HERE IS AN OLD SAYING, "There are many roads to Rome," and so it is with riding horses. The Olympics and World Championships can look very far away to a pony rider watching riders and horses jump huge fences in the various Grand Prix. Persistence is probably the most important trait for a rider to have. As Denny Emerson, the Olympic Three-Day Event rider, so aptly said, "You have to stick with it."

In riding there are good days, but there are also a lot of bad days. A thousand things can happen: a lame or sick horse, a judge doesn't like you, you miss all the distances. You have to be tough to take all that can go wrong, but the good days are thrilling. If the pressure of competing does not appeal to you, there are many other ways to enjoy riding horses: trail rides, fox hunts, and hunter paces to name a few.

However, if you are interested in competing, The American Horse Shows Association, 220 East 42nd Street, New York, NY, 10017-5806 (phone: 212-972-AHSA), is a good source of information about all disciplines. I urge all serious young riders to become members, as the AHSA offers a wealth of information about the sport. A second good source of information is *The Chronicle of the Horse*, a weekly magazine that is published in Middleburg, Virginia. *The Chronicle* prints summaries of all major events here and abroad, as well as articles of general interest. *The Chronicle* is an official publication of many organizations and can put you in touch with any of them: Masters of Foxhounds Association of America; United States Equestrian Team, Inc.; The United States Pony Clubs, Inc.; The National Riding Commission of the American Alliance of Health, Physical Education, Recreation and Dance; Foxhound Club of North America; Roster of Packs of the National Beagle Club of America, Inc.; United States Dressage Federation, Inc.; American Vaulting Association; North American Riding for the Handicapped Association, Inc.; and Intercollegiate Horse Show Association.

The two national organizations whose local chapters offer the best programs for young riders are the United States Pony Clubs, Inc., Kentucky Horse Park, 4071 Iron Works Pike, Lexington, KY 40511, and the 4-H Club of America, which you may reach through the Cooperative Extension 4-H Agent of any county in the United States. Your telephone book will have their number. Contact them directly for information about the chapters in your area.

Young riders living in the country may find a local fox hunt nearby. For information about fox hunts, contact the Masters of Foxhounds Association of America, 294 Washington Street, Room 851, Boston, MA 02108. Some of the best riders in the nation have come up through the ranks of Pony Club.

To the youngsters who wonder how to get from here to there, from where they are now to where they want to be in this sport, let me repeat Denny Emerson's encouraging words: "Somehow the really hungry ones will find a way. They will muck stalls for rides, they will wheedle rides, they will ride tough little creatures that no one else wants to get on. Their drive will win them through somehow, sooner or later, if they are dedicated enough."

For those who simply want to ride for pleasure, I say, "Just do it." There is no greater pleasure than a nice ride on a nice horse on a beautiful day. Even an ordinary ride is not all that bad. The old saying is true: "The outside of a horse is good for the inside of a man," or woman—no matter how young or old.

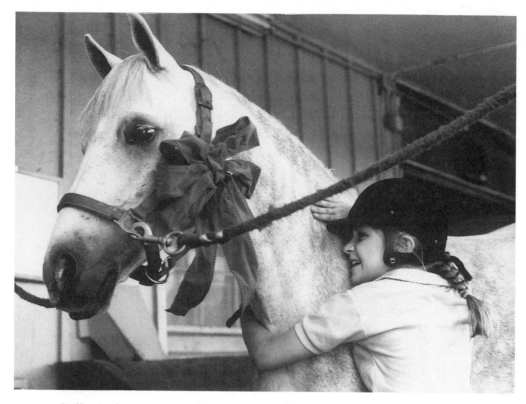

Cullen's dream was to have a pony of her own and that dream came true at Christmastime. She has gone on to her own bigger pony and to bigger jumps. She is on her way.

Afterword

From the Pony Himself

As you can see in the picture, Cullen is on her way. Her family bought a very lovely pony for her to show in the Medium Pony Division. I am only a little sad to see her move on. The most fun for me is starting riders out on the right track. "Well begun is half done," as the saying goes, is especially true of riding horses. So many people stop riding because as youngsters they had bad experiences with horses. If a child is bitten or kicked or bucked off or run away with, it is understandable that he or she will never want to be close to a horse again, let alone ride him.

I like to send my young riders "on to the next" with confidence and love of horses in their hearts. Whether they choose to ride in competition or simply for pleasure, I want them to enjoy riding horses for the rest of their lives, just as one of my early riders, Philip Richter, does. Right now

But already I have a darling new (and very young) rider, Phoebe.
She is only five years old, much younger than is usually permitted
at our barn. An exception was made for her because she is so very
keen. However, notice that the smaller the child, the more the
teacher has to be very careful there are no mishaps. Very small
children are better off starting in a western saddle so they can grasp
the horn if necessary.

Here I am sporting my makeshift (made from baling twine) overcheck to keep me from grabbing a bite of grass and losing this little girl over my head! Even the most well-behaved ponies find grass tempting.

Also very young children must be led or longed over a much longer period of time, and their "lessons" need to be shorter in time. A half-hour is the max, and often ten minutes is enough.

Cullen teaches Phoebe how to hold a "treat" for me. Keep your hand flat and all fingers together.

Looking back, one of my favorite riders and my owner still today, Philip Richter is shown here jumping in a horse show for the very first time. He was a real beginner then, but I knew how to get him around the course safely. Credit: Redwing.

Several years later, see how he has improved. We were a good team until he grew too tall for me. Credit: Tarrance.

Now, many years later, he rides well over big jumps. I'm proud of him and he is grateful to me for giving him such a good start. Credit: Pennington.

Why at age 25+ (75 in human years) I cannot retire yet. I want to teach all these young children how to ride. I love my "job" and never want to quit.

he loves to compete and show over huge jumps in the Amateur Owner Jumper Division, but I bet you a bag of carrots he will always enjoy riding even when he is an old man. As for me, I look forward to teaching the next young rider. Young riders keep me young. Good luck to all of you.

Your pal,

Frosty Lad

Index

(Entries in *italics* refer to illustrations)